FinTech Law and Policy

Lee Reiners

1st Edition

To Kate

Contents

Preface 4

Introduction – What is FinTech? 6

Chapter 1: The Evolving Relationship between FinTechs, Regulators, and Traditional Financial Institutions 10

    What Can Go Wrong When FinTechs Don't Understand Regulation 11

    Regulatory Challenges Facing U.S. Fintech Firms 13

    Evolution of FinTech in the U.S. 15

    Trends in FinTech Investment 18

    How FinTech Is Challenging Regulators around the Globe 21

    Regulatory Sandboxes 24

Chapter 2: FinTech Lending 26

    Explaining FinTech Credit 27

    U.S. and Global Landscape 31

    Regulatory and Legal Considerations 34

    Common Lending Models 36

    Vulnerabilities of FinTech Credit 40

    Additional Legal Considerations 43

Chapter 3: Banking Regulation in the United States 45

    Creating and Regulating a Bank 46

    Special Purpose FinTech Charter 51

    Industrial Loan Company Charter 54

Chapter 4: Cryptocurrency and Initial Coin Offerings 57

    Explaining Cryptocurrency 58

    Regulating Cryptocurrency as Money 63

    Regulating Cryptocurrency as a Commodity 66

    Regulating Cryptocurrency as Property 69

    Explaining Initial Coin Offerings 70

    Regulatory Framework for Initial Coin Offerings 73

Chapter 5: FinTech Payments, Wealth Management, and Account Aggregation 77

Traditional Payment Systems	78
Card Based Payments and Interbank Transfers	84
Mobile Payment Developments	90
Decentralized Payments	95
A Push for Faster Payments in the U.S.	97
Chapter 6: FinTech Wealth Management and Financial Account Aggregators	99
FinTech Wealth Management	100
Financial Account Aggregators	105
Acknowledgements	107
References	108

Preface

In 2016, few people had ever heard of Bitcoin or blockchain, initial coin offerings were non-existent, and U.S. financial regulatory agencies had yet to react to the emergence of nonbank financial services providers. The FinTech industry has changed dramatically since then: Bitcoin has captured the public imagination and spawned new derivatives products, you can apply for a mortgage on your smartphone, initial coin offerings are now a viable alternative to venture capital funding, and the Office of the Comptroller of the Currency has proposed a new kind of bank charter specifically for FinTech firms.

While many have focused on the technologies underpinning the FinTech revolution, less attention has been placed on how these technologies fit within the current financial regulatory framework. Understanding this framework is critical to the long-term success of any FinTech startup. While technology startups in other sectors may predicate their business on breaking rules and ignoring regulations, such a strategy is sure to fail if deployed by a FinTech firm. This is because the financial industry is heavily regulated by multiple state and federal agencies that often have overlapping authority. Being a successful FinTech firm requires more than just great technology; it also requires an understanding of the laws and regulations applicable to your business.

This book aims to provide you with that understanding. You will learn about the critical legal, regulatory, and policy issues associated with cryptocurrencies, initial coin offerings, online lending, new payments and wealth management technologies, and financial account aggregators. In addition, you will learn how regulatory agencies in the U.S. are continually adjusting to the emergence of new financial technologies and how the Office of the Comptroller of the Currency has proposed a path for FinTech firms to become regulated banks. If you are unfamiliar with how these new financial technologies work, fear not. Each chapter begins with a high-level overview of the underlying technology.

While this book is principally focused on the U.S. FinTech industry, it does not cover every relevant legal and regulatory issue. In addition, the regulatory framework applicable to various FinTech sectors is unsettled and constantly changing. Therefore, by the time you read this book, certain information may no longer be applicable or relevant. While future versions of the book will incorporate the most recent regulatory and legal developments, at no time should this book be construed as legal advice. Rather, the goal of the book is to familiarize you with the key legal and regulatory challenges that FinTech firms in various sectors face, as well as the critical policy debates that are occurring in Washington D.C. and state capitals across the country. Enjoy!

Introduction – What is FinTech?

"FinTech" is an amorphous term that is used differently depending on the context, but many people commonly think of FinTech as a relatively recent and unique marriage of financial services and information technology.[1] However, finance and technology have long gone together and supported each other, with financial firms supplying the capital to fund technological developments and then incorporating many of these new technologies into their business.

In fact, you could argue that one of the earliest examples of FinTech occurred in the mid-1800s, with the introduction of the telegraph and the laying of the first transcontinental telegraph line, which helped integrate the national economy. In 1871, ten years after the first transcontinental telegraph, Western Union introduced money transfers, making them arguably the country's first FinTech firm. A more recent FinTech example occurred in 1967 when Barclays introduced the automatic teller machine or ATM.

Thinking of FinTech as a recent phenomenon also ignores the fact that the financial industry has historically been the largest purchaser of information technology. The banking and securities industry spends over 7% of their annual revenue on IT [see Figure A] and the amount that large financial firms spend every year on IT is staggering. In 2016 alone, JPMorgan spent $9.5 billion dollars on technology.[2]

Figure A

IT Budget as a Percentage of Revenue

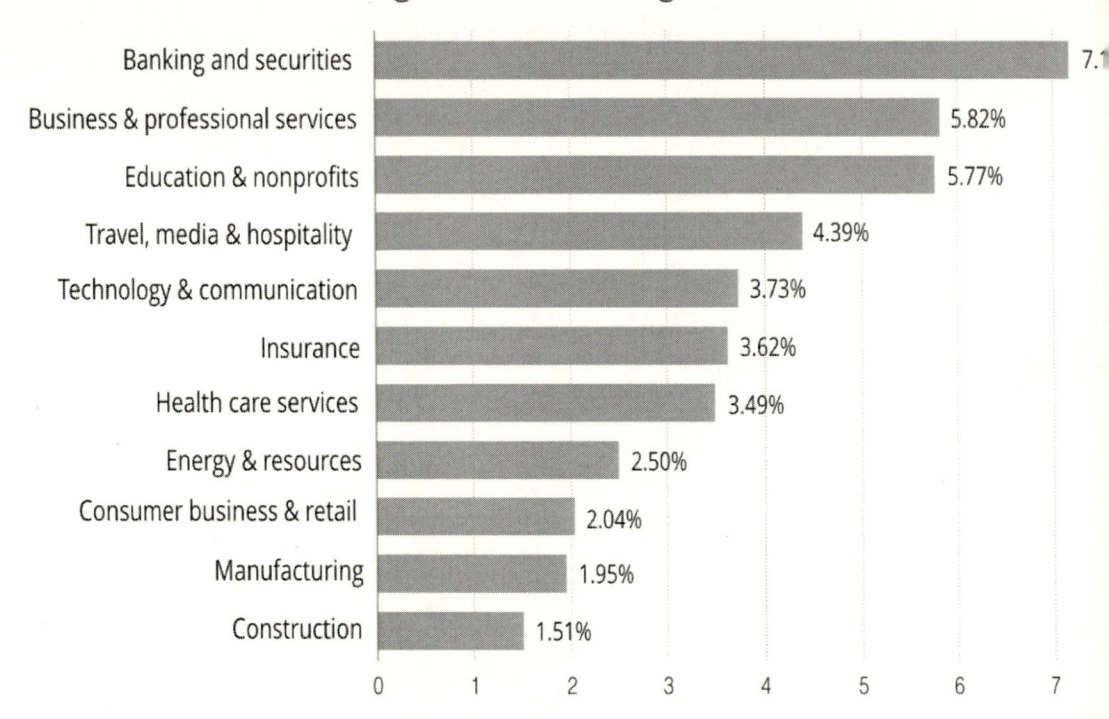

Industry	Percentage
Banking and securities	7.1
Business & professional services	5.82%
Education & nonprofits	5.77%
Travel, media & hospitality	4.39%
Technology & communication	3.73%
Insurance	3.62%
Health care services	3.49%
Energy & resources	2.50%
Consumer business & retail	2.04%
Manufacturing	1.95%
Construction	1.51%

Deloitte 2016-2017 Global CIO Survey, N=747

If the application of finance to technology is nothing new, why has FinTech generated so much buzz these past few years? The current hype and policy concerns arise not so much from the technology itself, but from who is applying the technology. Many FinTech firms are nonbank financial services companies. In other words, these firms are defined by what they are not, namely, banks.

The proliferation of these companies is assisted by rapid technological developments. The Internet has lowered many barriers to providing financial services. It is now possible for these types of companies to readily acquire customers without the need of a physical branch to accept deposits. It has also made these firms more competitive on a cost-basis and facilitated rapid expansion to national operations. Smart phones have also lowered barriers to using financial services. Just think, the first iPhone was introduced in 2007. Now, Pew Research reports that 77% of Americans own a smart phone – the functional equivalent of a bank branch in their pocket.[3] Our phones are capable of sending money to friends, depositing checks, and even buying stocks and other financial instruments. Distributed ledger technology holds the potential to seamlessly and securely transfer digital assets without the need for financial intermediaries.

In addition to technological advancements, modern FinTech was also spurred on by the 2008 financial crisis. It is hard to overstate the impact the crisis had on today's FinTech marketplace. Almost 9 million U.S. workers lost their job, many of whom were in the financial services industry.[4] Out of work, many of these people found their way to burgeoning FinTech companies. In addition, many tech-savvy college graduates were confronted with a lack of job opportunities, so they decided to start their own FinTech companies or join a recent startup. Congress also adopted tougher bank standards and regulations in response to the crisis. This increased compliance obligations for traditional banks and led them to pull back from certain business and market segments, which provided an opportunity for new FinTech firms to pick up market share.

Many consumers lost trust in traditional financial institutions after the crisis and rightfully so as many banks had to be bailed out by the government. In 2006, before the crisis, 30% of respondents in the General Social Survey indicated that they had a great deal of confidence in banks and financial institutions. Four years later, in 2010, only 11% of respondents had a great deal of confidence in banks and financial institutions.[5] Similar declines in consumer trust occurred in most major countries aside from China, which remained relatively insulated from the effects of the financial crisis. As a result, many consumers were more willing to engage with new technology startups who offered competing financial services products.

The financial crisis led consumers to not only lose trust in financial institutions, but in central banks and other government institutions as well. Many blame central banks and regulatory agencies for contributing to the crisis, or at least failing to prevent it. When governments around the world bailed out their banks, consumers were incredulous and those put out of work were left wondering where their bailout was. This loss of trust in governmental institutions gave rise to cryptocurrencies and other decentralized applications that were outside the government's control.

With all this in mind, I'd like to narrow the definition of FinTech by describing it in two parts. First, the term refers to businesses who are using technology to operate outside of traditional financial services business models to change how financial services are offered. Second, FinTech includes firms that use technology to improve the competitive advantage of traditional financial services firms by providing faster and more convenient products and services to their customers.

The first part of the definition refers to those nonbank technology companies that have entered into the financial services space, while the second part of the definition applies to legacy financial institutions who are deploying and developing innovative new technologies.

This definition also implies that FinTech covers the entire range of products and services that have historically been provided by financial services firms. This book will focus on the FinTech activities that will likely have the greatest impact on the future of finance. This includes: online lending, cryptocurrencies, initial coin offerings, payments, wealth management, and account aggregation.

Chapter 1: The Evolving Relationship between FinTechs, Regulators, and Traditional Financial Institutions

What Can Go Wrong When FinTechs Don't Understand Regulation

The following examples highlight what can happen when FinTech firms fail to comply with applicable rules and regulations. My intention is not to shame or single out these companies, but rather to emphasize the importance and necessity for FinTech firms to incorporate legal and regulatory considerations into their product design and decision making from the very beginning. Doing so can save a lot of time, money, and headache down the road.

The first examples are from the FinTech lending industry. In 2008, online lending platform Prosper, which connects borrowers with lenders online, received a cease-and-desist order from the Securities and Exchange Commission (SEC), who stated that Prosper was an unregistered seller of securities.[6] The order arose from how Prosper was funding their loans. Rather than have the lenders, or investors, buy the loans outright, Prosper was selling these investors notes whose payment stream depended on the borrowers making their loan payments on time and in whole. The SEC determined that these notes were technically securities that needed to be registered with the SEC.[1]

More recently, in April 2018, online lender Lending Club was fined two million dollars by the Massachusetts Division of Banks for making more than 46,000 loans in the state without a proper state license.[7] This fine was related to a 2011 consent order in which the division stripped Lending Club's license for charging borrower's fees that violated Massachusetts small-loan laws.[8]

Moving on to the world of payments, in 2015, PayPal agreed to pay $7.7 million dollars in a settlement with the Office of Foreign Assets Control, which is the U.S. Department of the Treasury's sanctions enforcement arm, for processing 486 illegal transactions, totaling approximately $44,000, that violated sanctions on Sudan, Cuba and Iran.[9] Also in 2015, The Financial Crimes Enforcement Network (FinCEN) assessed a $700,000 civil money penalty against Ripple Labs Inc. and its wholly-owned subsidiary, XRP II LLC for willfully violating several requirements of the Bank Secrecy Act (BSA).[10]

There are numerous examples of cryptocurrency firms running afoul of the law and regulations. In 2014, the founder of online Bitcoin exchange, BitInstant, pled guilty to operating an unlicensed money transmitting business, through which he knowingly transmitted money intended to facilitate criminal activity, specifically drug trafficking on Silk Road, a black market website designed to enable its users to buy and sell illegal drugs anonymously and beyond the reach of law enforcement.[11] In 2015, the Commodity Futures Trading Commission (CFTC) settled charges against online facility Derivabit and its founder for offering Bitcoin options contracts without complying with the Commodity

---

[1] Prosper subsequently did register with the SEC.

Exchange Act and CFTC regulations.[12] In February 2018, the SEC charged Bitcoin exchange BitFunder and its founder for operating an unregistered securities exchange and defrauding users of that exchange by misappropriating their Bitcoins and failing to disclose a cyber-attack on BitFunder's system that resulted in the theft of more than 6,000 Bitcoins.[13]

The initial coin offering market is also ripe with fraud, or more generously, actors who ignore or are unfamiliar with applicable laws and regulations. In January 2018, the SEC seized the assets of self-described decentralized banking platform AriseBank, and subsequently charged the founders with fraud.[14] AriseBank allegedly raised $600 million dollars in an initial coin offering by claiming that it had developed an algorithmic trading application that automatically trades in various cryptocurrencies and falsely stated that it had purchased an FDIC insured bank, which enabled it to offer customers FDIC insured accounts. In December 2017, Munchee Incorporated, a California based company selling digital tokens to investors for its blockchain based food review service, halted its ICO after being contacted by the SEC's cyber-unit, and agreed to an order that found their conduct constituted unregistered securities offers and sales.[15] The company had promoted the offering as a utility token, but still told investors that the tokens would rise in value due to the efforts of others and a secondary market would be created.

Hopefully, these examples emphasize the importance of getting regulation right, and what can happen when FinTech firms get it wrong. In the most severe cases, getting it wrong spells the end of the company. FinTech companies that begin operating with a firm grasp of the laws and regulations applicable to their business can not only avoid the pitfalls that have ensnared many a FinTech before them, but also gain a competitive advantage and make the company a more attractive investment for venture capital firms and other potential investors.

Regulatory Challenges Facing U.S. Fintech Firms

The U.S. financial regulatory structure is complex, and it can challenge even the most sophisticated FinTech firm's ability to identify the regulations with which they must comply. The core issue is regulatory oversight in the United States is fragmented across multiple regulators at the federal level, and many FinTechs will also have to deal with regulatory bodies in the states they wish to do business in. Adding to the confusion, many of the regulations implemented and overseen by these federal and state agencies were developed long before the type of product or service FinTech firms are now offering existed.

As you might imagine, navigating this complex web of regulation takes time and is costly. The cost of researching applicable laws and regulations can be particularly significant for FinTech firms that begin as technology startups with small staffs and limited venture capital funding. One of the biggest costs for FinTech firms seeking to operate nationwide is the cost to obtain state licenses. FinTech payments and lending firms that are not subject to routine federal oversight must typically obtain state licenses. The Government Accountability Office estimates that obtaining all state licenses generally costs FinTech payments firms and FinTech lenders $1 million to $30 million, which includes legal fees, state bonds, and direct regulatory costs.[16]

There are also costs associated with being examined. Because most FinTech firms operate in multiple states, it is possible for a single FinTech firm to be examined multiple times a year by various state regulatory agencies. Examinations impose costs on FinTech firms by way of time and resources that otherwise could have been spent on growing the business.

These challenges are not unique to FinTech firms. But what does make FinTech firms different is that they typically seek to operate in multiple states, or nationwide, at their inception. Historically, money transmitters or nonbank lenders got their start in a limited geographic area and therefore, only had to obtain a license in one state. As their business grew, they may have expanded into additional states and obtained licenses in those states, but they were able to spread the cost of getting these licenses over time. For a FinTech firm, obtaining a license in multiple states at inception can eat into limited venture capital funding and divert critical resources away from the task of building the business.

FinTech firms also face uncertainty when it comes to how their product is regulated and how regulation may change. FinTech lenders for instance, must contend with multiple agencies who have authorities related to consumer protection and fair lending. The Federal Trade Commission and Consumer Financial Protection Bureau can take enforcement actions against nonbank FinTech firms for violations of any federal consumer protection laws they enforce, and they may have different interpretations of what conduct merits consumer protection enforcement actions. One specific area where this creates uncertainty is in the use of nontraditional data by FinTech lenders to assess borrower creditworthiness. Many FinTech lenders are concerned that the use of this data may produce outcomes that violate fair lending laws and regulations.

Companies that aggregate information pertaining to a consumer's financial accounts, like Mint, face uncertainty as to which party will bear responsibility for unauthorized transactions. Will it be the aggregator, or will it be the bank or other financial institution where the customer holds their account?

There is also significant uncertainty as to whether or not it's possible to structure an initial coin offering (ICO) inn such a way that it avoids being classified as a security subject to SEC registration. The SEC has yet to offer definitive guidance on the status of ICOs, choosing instead to take enforcement actions where clear violations of securities laws have occurred.

The costs and uncertainty imposed by the U.S.' fragmented regulatory structure has led many FinTech firms to reassess their business strategy. The idealism present in the early days of the modern FinTech moment, circa 2008, has given way to a more pragmatic approach whereby the goal of many FinTech firms now is to partner with, or be acquired by, a traditional financial institution. This goal is more easily accomplished when the FinTech firm has a strong record of regulatory compliance.

Evolution of FinTech in the U.S.

Why have we yet to see some version of Uber or Airbnb disrupt the banking industry? Before you answer that question, think about how these two companies got to where they're at today. When Uber wanted to operate in New York City, did they go to the New York City taxi and limousine commission and ask for permission? Same for Airbnb, did they seek a hotel license to operate in each city? Of course not! These two companies identified a market need, built a product to meet this need, and then released it to the public. Consumers flocked to these products because they were far superior to anything else out there, and government agencies around the world were left with little choice but to accommodate these new products, lest they provoke their citizenry.

So again, why hasn't something like Uber or Airbnb happened in the banking industry? Is it because most of us are generally satisfied with our current bank and therefore there is no market need? Given the lack of consumer trust in the financial industry, especially since the financial crisis, I would say the answer is no. The real reason is that the banking industry is fundamentally different from any other industry because you're dealing with people's money. Along with that, comes a high degree of regulation by multiple regulatory agencies at the federal and state level.

In essence, the Uber and Airbnb mentality of "it is better to ask for forgiveness than permission" simply does not work in finance. This does not mean that some FinTechs haven't aspired to be the Uber or Airbnb of finance. After all, many of the technologists at the forefront of the FinTech boom are cut from the same cloth as those that ushered in the sharing economy, adhering to the Silicon Valley mantra of "move fast and break things." These people are risk takers, who spend little time thinking about, and have little regard for, regulations. Some of these early FinTech firms sought to deploy their products and services before regulators had a chance to understand exactly how the product worked and how it fit into the existing regulatory regime. This method does have its advantages, mainly that consumers might actually enjoy the product and benefit from its use. This puts pressure on the regulators not to intervene too aggressively. But of course, this strategy also carries significant risk – the biggest being that one or more regulatory agencies shuts the company down for good.

As time has gone on and regulatory agencies have increasingly exerted their authority, FinTech innovators have come to understand that disrupting any aspect of finance is no easy task. This reality has led to a shift in mentality within the FinTech industry from disruption to partnership. Now, the stated goal of many new FinTech firms is to partner with, or be acquired by, a traditional financial institution. We can see this fact reflected in figure 1.1, which shows how venture capital funds are cashing out of their investments in FinTech companies. The most common way for venture capital funds to exit their FinTech investments is through a strategic acquisition, meaning that the FinTech company they've invested in was purchased by a financial institution or possibly even a larger FinTech company. The number of strategic acquisitions has been steadily increasing and reached a peak in 2017 with fifty-nine.

Figure 1.1

Global Venture-Backed Exit Activity by Type (#) in FinTech

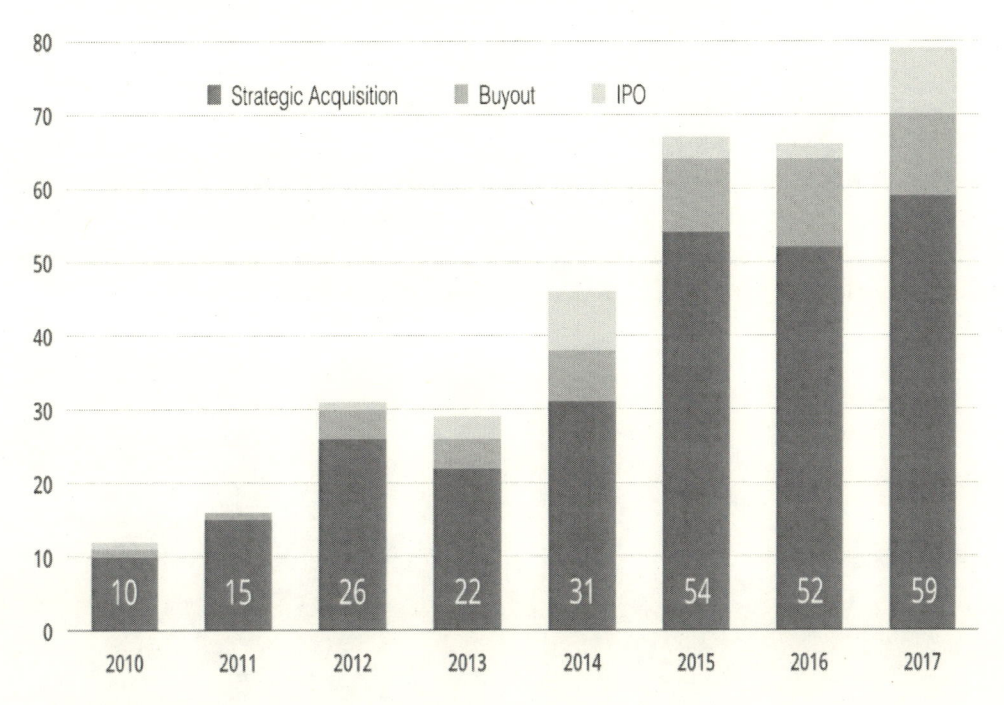

Year	Total
2010	10
2011	15
2012	26
2013	22
2014	31
2015	54
2016	52
2017	59

Source: Pulse of FinTech Q4'17 Global Analysis of Investment in FinTech, KPMG International (Data provided by PitchBook)

Even with this growth in strategic acquisitions, it is not easy for a FinTech to be purchased by, or even partner with, a traditional financial institution. In a 2017 survey, global consulting firm PwC asked FinTech companies and financial institutions what the biggest challenges were when it came to working with one another.[17] For financial institutions, the biggest challenge in working with FinTech companies is IT security. This makes sense given how tightly regulated traditional financial institutions are and the expectation of regulators and customers that the institution appropriately safeguard customer data. For financial institutions, a major data breach could seriously threaten the ongoing viability of the firm. When FinTech companies were asked what challenges they faced in working with financial institutions, the most common answer given was "differences in management and culture." This answer also makes sense given the more freewheeling culture within tech startups, which contrasts sharply with the button-down, hierarchical structure of many financial institutions.

Banks are also going to be more naturally cautious when it comes to working with FinTech firms because they are liable for risks posed by third-parties. This means that banks will spend significant amounts of time conducting due diligence on the practices and controls in place at FinTech firms seeking to partner with them in order to prevent unnecessary compliance or operational risks. Small banks with fewer resources to dedicate to due diligence may be unwilling to risk partnering with FinTech firms. Bank due diligence can lead to lengthy delays in establishing partnerships, which can put FinTech firms at risk of going out of business if they do not have sufficient funding on-hand and are unable to access new customers on their own.

Despite these challenges, a bank-FinTech partnership can be mutually beneficial. For banks, partnering with a FinTech can allow them to offer greater consumer choice and a better customer experience, along with potentially lowering costs through the more efficient use of new technologies. For FinTechs, partnering with a bank provides access to customers, financial resources, and regulatory expertise. Nevertheless, expect to see more bank-FinTech partnerships in the years ahead.

Trends in FinTech Investment

Figure 1.2 shows the growth in global investment activity in FinTech companies by quarter, dating back to 2010. This includes investment from venture capital funds, private equity funds, and investment through mergers and acquisitions. There was steady growth in the years immediately after the financial crisis and this growth peaked in the fourth quarter of 2015, with $24.8 billion dollars in new investment. FinTech investment activity has cooled off significantly since then in terms of deal value, but the number of new deals closing every quarter has remained relatively stable, with over 300 new deals closing every quarter since the beginning of 2014. Figure 1.3 shows that U.S. investment activity in FinTech companies has followed a similar trend, with the value of new deals peaking in the fourth quarter of 2015.

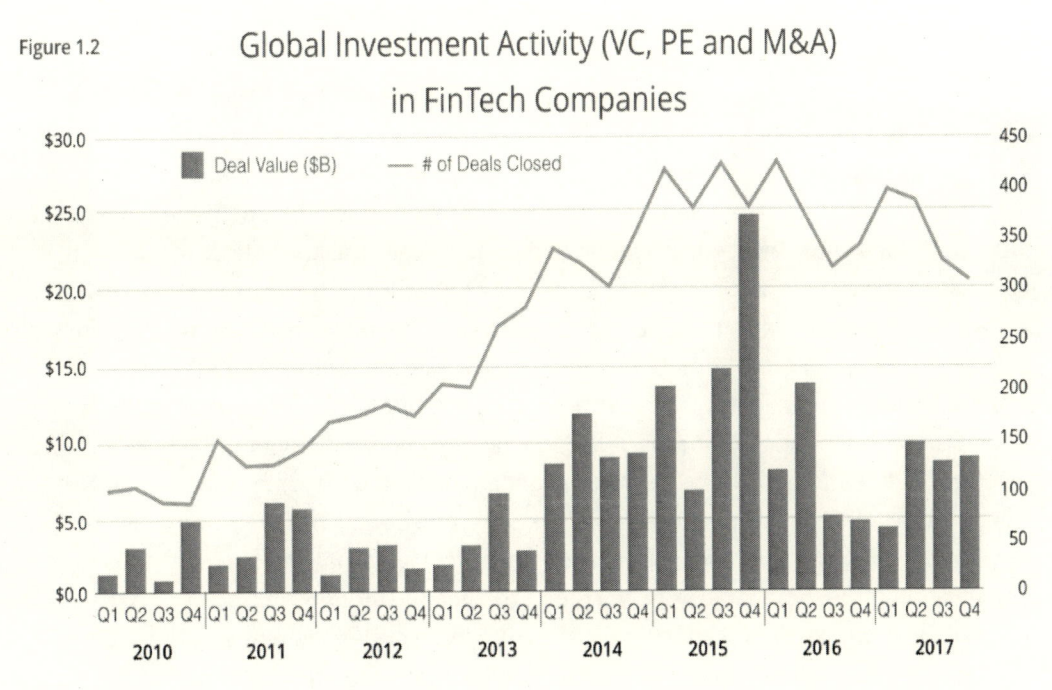

Figure 1.2

Global Investment Activity (VC, PE and M&A) in FinTech Companies

Source: Pulse of FinTech Q4'17 Global Analysis of Investment in FinTech, KPMG International. (Data provided by PitchBook)

Figure 1.3

Total U.S. Investment Activity (VC, PE and M&A) in FinTech Companies

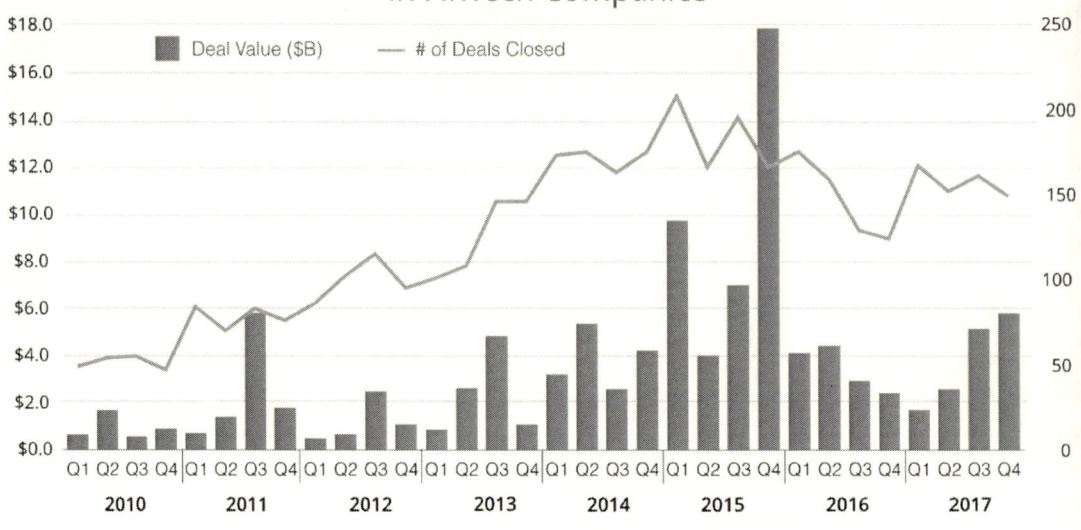

Deal Value ($B) — # of Deals Closed

Source: Pulse of FinTech Q4'17 Global Analysis of Investment in FinTech, KPMG International (Data provided by PitchBook)

The fact that the value of new investments flowing into FinTech companies has come down considerably since 2015 while the overall number of new deals has remained stable reflects a decrease in FinTech company valuations that corresponds to the shift in mentality within the FinTech industry from disruption to partnership. In the FinTech industry's early years after the financial crisis, there was considerable optimism that FinTech would transform financial services the way Amazon transformed retail or Uber transformed transportation. This optimism was aided by buzzwords like blockchain, which was promoted as a revolutionary new technology that would fundamentally alter the finance industry and eventually the entire economy, but which few people actually understood. This hype and optimism led to a flood of new money pouring into the FinTech industry, but when many of these freshly funded FinTech companies failed to deliver the hoped for results, investor sentiment returned to more realistic levels and new investment activity cooled off. This has led many to argue that the FinTech industry is going through the hype cycle, a term coined by the consulting firm Gartner, to reflect the maturity and adoption of new technologies. The hype cycle [see figure 1.4] is a visual representation of the fact that we tend to overestimate the effect of a new technology in the short run and underestimate the effect in the long run. Thus, according to hype cycle terminology, 2015 may have been the peak of inflated expectations for the FinTech industry. While it is hard to say with certainty where we're currently at in the hype cycle, it is fair to assume that in the long-run, FinTech will prove to be a disruptive force in all aspects of finance.

Figure 1.4

Gartner Hype Cycle

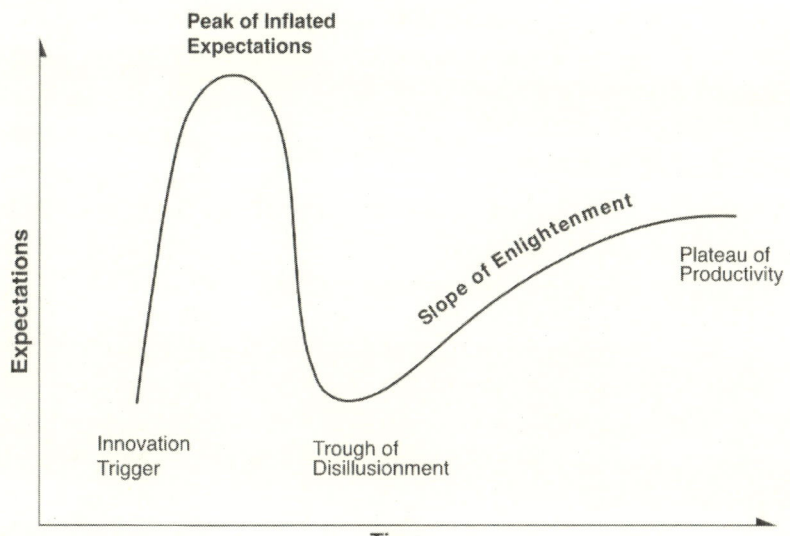

Source: Hype Cycle provided by Gartner, Inc.

How FinTech Is Challenging Regulators around the Globe

The FinTech industry is still young and has grown at an exceptional speed. This has placed pressure on financial regulators around the world to understand these new technologies and how they fit within the current regulatory framework. The pace of technological change necessitates a rethinking of current regulatory structures. These structures are largely premised on a model of banking that predates the digital revolution, a time when you conducted your banking at a local branch and balanced your checkbook every week. Regulations built for this model of banking are simply not conducive to fostering and promoting new innovations in financial services.

But how should regulators respond? Well, that depends on the jurisdiction. There are a variety of financial ecosystems around the world, all with varying degrees of complexity and regulatory frameworks. Given this diversity, there is not going to be a one-size-fits-all approach that will work in every country, or satisfy all stakeholders in each country. Different regulatory agencies may also have different mentalities when it comes to innovation and these mentalities will play a large role in how they respond to FinTech. In some countries, like the U.K. for instance, regulators are tasked with promoting competition and these regulators may view FinTech firms as being better situated to meet the needs of market segments that are not currently being served by traditional banks. Many regulatory agencies also recognize that technology is, and will remain, a part of life and if that consumers are utilizing financial services in new and innovative ways, it is incumbent upon them to adjust and accommodate these new technologies. Regulatory agencies are also responding on the basis of inquiries from industry stakeholders. Many new FinTech firms have begun asking how they are regulated, placing the regulator in the position of having to determine what adjustments in current frameworks are needed, if any, to accommodate the various changes occurring in the business operations and models within the financial services space.

Complicating the U.S. response to FinTech is a fragmented regulatory system, with FinTech activity often being supervised by two or more regulatory agencies. Each of these agencies has a different statutory mandate and internal culture, and may not see eye to eye on many issues, including FinTech. Absent a comprehensive national FinTech strategy, several U.S. federal regulatory agencies have adopted their own initiatives that are primarily designed to facilitate communication between FinTech innovators and financial regulators. For instance, the Consumer Financial Protection Bureau (CFPB) has launched Project Catalyst, which is an initiative to encourage consumer-friendly developments for consumer financial products and services.[18] Through Project Catalyst, the CFPB has launched several research collaborations with companies that are testing financial products or services. Through these projects, the CFPB gains insight into how consumers make financial decisions and improve their understanding of new consumer friendly innovations in the marketplace. According to the CFPB, as of August 2017, they had met with approximately 150 companies in four project catalyst events in New York and San Francisco.

The Commodity Futures Trading Commission (CFTC) launched Lab CFTC to be the hub for the agency's engagement with the FinTech innovation community.[19] It is designed to make the CFTC more accessible to FinTech innovators, and serve as a platform to inform the commission's understanding of new technologies. Lab CFTC's core components include "Guidepoint" – a dedicated point of contact for FinTech innovators to engage with the CFTC, learn about the CFTC's regulatory framework, and obtain feedback and information on the implementation of innovative technology ideas for the market – and "CFTC 2.0" – a program to foster and help initiate the adoption of new technology within the CFTC's own mission activities through collaboration with FinTech industry and CFTC market participants.

The Office of the Comptroller of the Currency, or OCC, launched the Office of Innovation to be the central contact and clearinghouse for requests and information relating to innovation in the federal banking system.[20] The Office of Innovation has four core components: 1) outreach and technical assistance to establish open and continuing dialogue with banks, financial technology companies and other nonbank parties and technical assistance; 2) coordination and facilitation to implement a process to streamline and coordinate innovation related decisions to ensure transparent and timely responses to inquiries; 3) awareness and training that improves the skills and knowledge of OCC staff; and 4) research that assess the landscape and trends in financial innovation.

In addition to launching their own initiatives, U.S. regulatory agencies have also opened new channels to share information with one another in an effort to provide a more coordinated response to FinTech innovations. For example, in 2010, the Federal Reserve banks of Atlanta and Boston created the Mobile Payments Industry Working Group, to facilitate discussions among industry stakeholders about how a successful mobile payment system could evolve in the United States.[21] This group also functions as an inter-agency collaboration mechanism, through bi-annual meetings between industry stakeholders and relevant regulators.

In 2016, the Treasury Department created the Interagency Working Group on Marketplace Lending, which met three times over the course of fiscal year 2016.[22] The purpose of the working group was to share information, engage industry participants and public interest groups, and evaluate where additional regulatory clarity could protect borrowers and investors.

In March of 2017, the Federal Reserve convened the Interagency FinTech Discussion Forum, which is an informal group that meets approximately every four to six weeks and aims to facilitate information sharing among consumer compliance staff from the federal banking regulators on FinTech consumer protection issues and supervisory outcomes.[23] Discussion topics have included account aggregation, alternative data, modeling techniques, as well as third-party oversight.

In addition to these domestic interagency working groups, there are a number of FinTech collaboration efforts between regulators from different countries. Sharing information across regulatory agencies, both domestic and foreign, allows regulators to stay abreast of the latest FinTech developments and can promote a common understanding and consistent application of laws and regulations.

Regulatory Sandboxes

Regulators abroad have addressed the emergence of financial innovation through various means, including: establishing innovation offices, establishing mechanisms for allowing FinTech firms to conduct trial operations, holding innovation competitions, providing funding for firms through business accelerators, and using various methods to coordinate with other regulators domestically and internationally.

One of the more common approaches that's emerged is what's known as a regulatory sandbox, which exist in over a dozen countries and can be thought of as a safe space in which businesses can test innovative products, services, business models and delivery mechanisms without immediately incurring all the normal regulatory consequences of engaging in these activities. At a basic level, a sandbox works through the following four steps: 1) FinTech firms apply to participate; 2) if accepted by the regulator, the firm agrees with the regulator on the parameters of how products or services will be tested, such as the number of consumers or transactions included in the test, or the timeframe of the test; 3) the firm secures the appropriate licenses, if applicable, and begins testing their product; and 4) the firm and regulators interact regularly throughout the testing process.

The first regulatory agency to launch a FinTech sandbox was the United Kingdom's Financial Conduct Authority (FCA). The FCA is the conduct regulator for financial services firms and financial markets in the UK and they have a specific mandate to promote effective competition in the interest of consumers, which is what drove their decision to launch the sandbox. The FCA stated they launched the sandbox in order to: reduce the time and cost of getting innovative ideas to market; enable greater access to funding for innovators; allow more products to be tested and introduced into the market; ensure appropriate consumer protection safeguards are built into new products and services; and facilitate better outcomes for consumers.[24] The FCA was also concerned about national competitiveness, and launched the sandbox to help the UK maintain its status as Europe's leading FinTech Hub.

In order for a firm to be admitted into the FCA's sandbox, they must prove that their product is a genuine innovation that would offer an identifiable benefit to consumers and is ready to be tested. Firms admitted into the sandbox may receive several possible benefits. The most sought after is a restricted authorization to operate. Any firm seeking to provide consumer financial services in the U.K. must be authorized or registered by the FCA, unless certain exemptions apply. The FCA created a tailored authorization process for firms accepted into the sandbox, whereby any authorization or registration will be restricted to allow firms to test only their ideas as agreed upon with the FCA.

Sandbox firms may also receive individual guidance, whereby the FCA clarifies rules and regulations that apply to the product being tested, or a waiver or modification to existing rules if the firm is concerned that their product being tested may breach one of the FCA's rules. The FCA would only grant a waiver or modification if they felt the rule is unduly burdensome or not achieving its purpose.

The final possible benefit for sandbox firms is referred to as a no enforcement action letter, which is an agreement between the firm and the FCA that provided the firm kept to the agreed upon testing parameters and treated customers fairly, the FCA accepts that unexpected issues may arise and would not expect to take disciplinary action.

The U.S.' fragmented regulatory structure makes implementing a FCA type of sandbox impossible – there are ten federal agencies involved in the regulation of FinTech in some capacity in the United States. Furthermore, unlike the FCA, most U.S. financial regulators do not have a mandate to promote competition or the authority to initiate a sandbox program.

Despite these hurdles, some federal agencies have adopted various elements of a regulatory sandbox. For instance, in 2017, the Consumer Financial Protection Bureau issued a No Action Letter to Upstart Network, a company that uses alternative data to assess creditworthiness and underwrite loans.[25] As part of the Letter, the CFPB agreed they would not recommend initiation of supervisory or enforcement action against Upstart with respect to the Equal Credit Opportunity Act provided that Upstart regularly reports lending and compliance information to the CFPB to mitigate risk to consumers and informs the CFPB about the impact of alternative data on lending decisions. The Securities and Exchange Commission and the Commodity Futures Trading Commission have also issued no action letters to FinTech firms.

While the hurdles to implementing a national FinTech regulatory sandbox are high, several states have debated launching their own form of sandbox, and in March of 2018, Arizona became the first U.S. state to do so. At the time, Arizona's governor, Doug Ducey said that "FinTech is going to fundamentally transform banking, finance and technology. We're going to be the first in the state to embrace it."[26]

Arizona's sandbox is administered by the state Attorney General's Office and is open to businesses bringing new products to market for activities that would normally require licenses issued by Arizona's Department of Financial Institutions, such as mortgage lending, consumer lending, and money transmission. FinTech companies in the Arizona sandbox will be able to test their products for up to two years, and serve as many as 10,000 customers before needing to apply for formal licensure.[27] Expect more states to follow Arizona's lead.

Chapter 2: FinTech Lending

Explaining FinTech Credit

FinTech credit encompasses all credit activity facilitated by electronic platforms whereby borrowers are matched directly with lenders. FinTech credit is also referred to as loan-based crowd funding, peer-to-peer lending, or marketplace lending. Whenever one of these terms is used, it's typically referring to the same thing – mainly some type of FinTech credit provision

These electronic platforms can facilitate a range of credit obligations including secured and unsecured lending to both businesses and consumers, as well as non-loan debt funding, such as invoice financing, which is simply a way for businesses to borrow money against the amounts due to them from customers. The platforms can also go beyond a peer-to-peer matching business model by using their own balance sheet to fund loans that they make and then keep these loans on their balance sheet.

There are several factors driving the supply of new FinTech credit providers and credit products. The most important factor is that FinTech lenders are able to make more intensive and efficient use of new digital innovations. They've been able to essentially automate the entire lending process which provides consumers with a convenient and quick service. In addition, FinTech lenders have been able to make use of new, non-traditional, data sources. To assess borrower credit risk, banks have traditionally relied on metrics like credit scores as well as debt and income levels. However, FinTech lenders are able to incorporate additional data elements, such as a business's sales volume on Amazon or eBay, or customer reviews from websites like Yelp. For assessing an individual's credit risk, FinTech lenders may incorporate data from social media profiles. Combined with traditional metrics, these additional data points may provide FinTech lenders with a more complete credit risk profile for each prospective borrower.

Figure 2.1 highlights the difference between banks and FinTech lenders credit scoring methodology. The data comes from online lender Lending Club, and it tracks the correlation over time between a borrower's FICO score, commonly referred to as your credit score, and the rating that Lending Club assigned to the borrower using their proprietary algorithm, which looks beyond FICO scores to estimate the likelihood of default. In Lending Club's early days in 2007, the correlation between the two was fairly high, at around 80%, but as time has gone on, and Lending Club has incorporated additional data points into their algorithm, the correlation has gone down quite significantly, to the point where in 2015, the correlation between a borrowers FICO score and the grade assigned to them by Lending Club was a little over 35%. This indicates that FinTech lenders, like Lending Club, continue to incorporate additional information into their credit scoring methodology, which is resulting in different borrower credit risk profiles than what a traditional bank would come up with. This holds the potential for borrowers who can't get access to credit from traditional banks because they have poor, or non-existent, credit scores, to get credit from FinTech lenders who are willing and able to look beyond the traditional credit score.

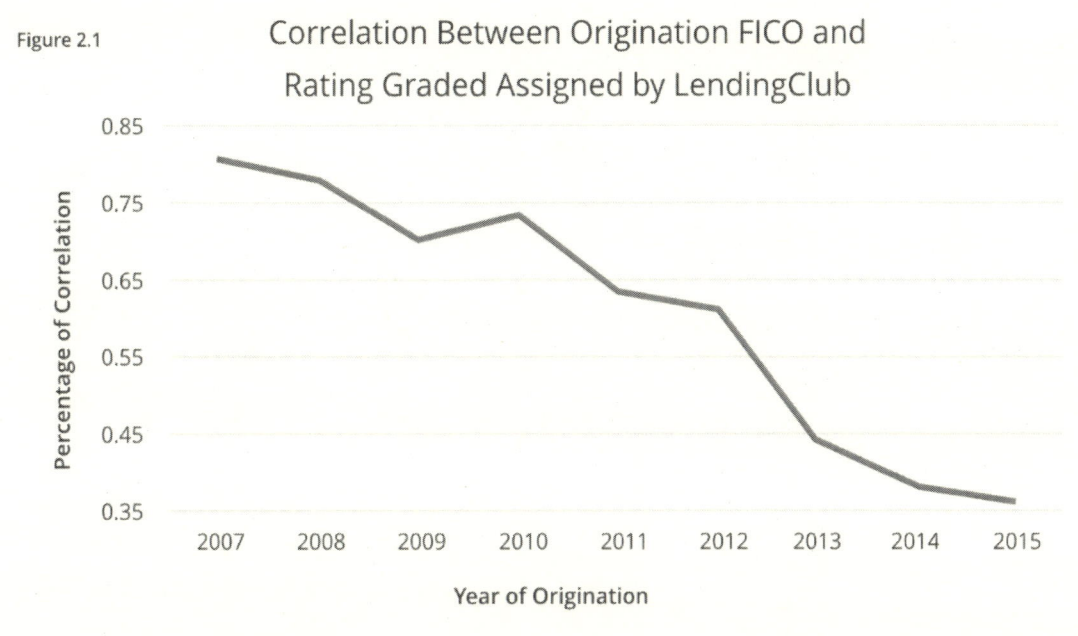

Figure 2.1

Correlation Between Origination FICO and Rating Graded Assigned by LendingClub

Percentage of Correlation (y-axis: 0.35 to 0.85)
Year of Origination (x-axis: 2007 to 2015)

FinTech Lending: Financial Inclusion, Risk Pricing, and Alternative Information; Federal Reserve Bank of Philadelphia

Another factor that's influencing the supply of FinTech credit is the ease with which FinTech lenders are able to scale. Once they've built the platform, the cost associated with acquiring the next customer is relatively low. Because everything is done digitally and online, FinTech lenders can reach a broad customer base. Because the lending process is automated there is minimal human intervention, which allows these FinTech lenders to grow quickly.

FinTech lenders also enjoy cost advantages over traditional lenders. FinTech lenders don't have brick and mortar branches to pay for and they're not wedded to legacy IT systems that are often costly to maintain. In addition, because most FinTech lenders are not banks and therefore not subject to supervision by federal banking agencies, they don't have to hold as much capital and liquidity as do banks and their overall regulatory compliance costs are lower.

The final factor that's driving the supply of new FinTech credit providers is that after the financial crisis, traditional lenders withdrew from certain market segments, either because they suffered heavy losses in these markets or because new rules and regulations imposed after the crisis made it no longer profitable to serve these segments, and this has created an opportunity for FinTech lenders to step in and fill that void. It is this potential for FinTech lenders to expand access to credit for underserved populations that has generated a lot of excitement around the industry, particularly amongst policymakers.

Small businesses are one of the groups that have experienced difficulty in obtaining credit in the wake of the financial crisis. While bank loans to bigger corporations have recovered since the recession, small business lending still hasn't caught up with levels from before the financial crisis [see figure 2.2.] This is in part because banks suffered particularly heavy losses on small business loans during the recession and remain wary of the sector. In addition, the cost of underwriting such loans can be prohibitive because of the time required for data collection and verification on what are often relatively small loan amounts. New online FinTech lenders, with their emphasis on automation, are helping to speed up the process and cut these costs. This is why many new FinTech lenders target small businesses exclusively.

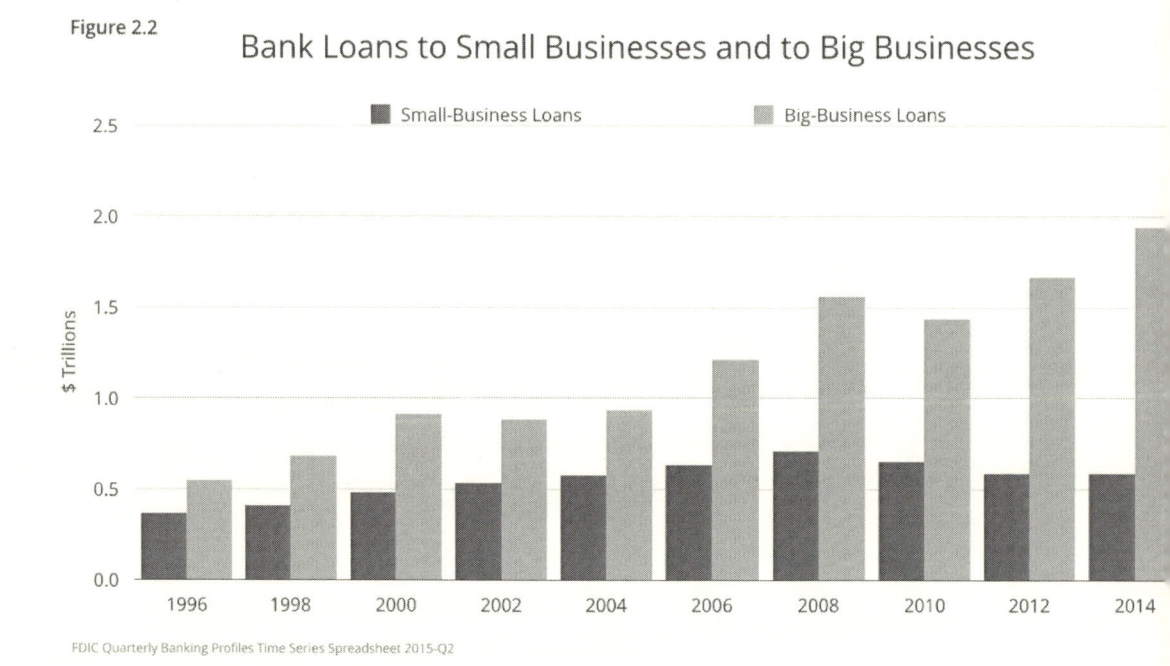

Figure 2.2

Bank Loans to Small Businesses and to Big Businesses

FDIC Quarterly Banking Profiles Time Series Spreadsheet 2015-Q2

The growth in FinTech credit is also being driven by several demand factors. Perhaps the biggest demand factor is changing consumer tastes and preferences. Nowadays, consumers expect a user-friendly experience as well as something that is convenient, fast, and cost effective, and this is something that FinTech lenders have thus far been successful at.

Changing demographic factors are also influencing the demand for FinTech credit products. There's an entire generation of young people, known as digital natives, that have spent their entire lives with access to the internet or mobile devices and have become accustom to doing everything online, including their banking. In addition, consumers in many emerging markets have rapidly adopted new digital technologies and these countries may not have a well-established banking system which creates an opportunity for FinTech credit providers to gain access to new customers with few competitors standing in their way.

Another factor influencing the demand of FinTech credit products is the decline in consumer trust in traditional lenders in the aftermath of the financial crisis. There may be a more general perception among some consumers, particularly young consumers, that FinTech lenders are more socially responsible and have greater social value than conventional banks and therefor they're more willing to engage with FinTech lenders.

The final factor influencing the demand for FinTech credit is the willingness of investors to purchase the loans generated by FinTech credit platforms. Without investors, FinTech lenders cannot make loans, because these lenders do not have enough capital to hold the loans on their own balance sheet. In the wake of the financial crisis, the Federal Reserve pushed interest rates to near zero, which lowered the returns investors were earning on traditional fixed-income assets, like corporate bonds. Tired of these low returns, many investors starting purchasing the loans being generated by FinTech credit platforms because they offered higher returns. This provided a boost to the nascent FinTech credit industry, but now that interest rates are starting to go up, many are wondering if investor appetite for FinTech loans will decline.

U.S. and Global Landscape

Figure 2.3 tracks the launch of new online nonbank lending platforms in the U.S.. Activity really started to take off around 2012 and peaked in 2014, when 14 new FinTech lending platforms were launched. In subsequent years, that activity has come down quite a bit, and this is on par with the other trends we've seen in the broader FinTech industry, not just when it comes to lending. It may be indicative of the market having become overly saturated.

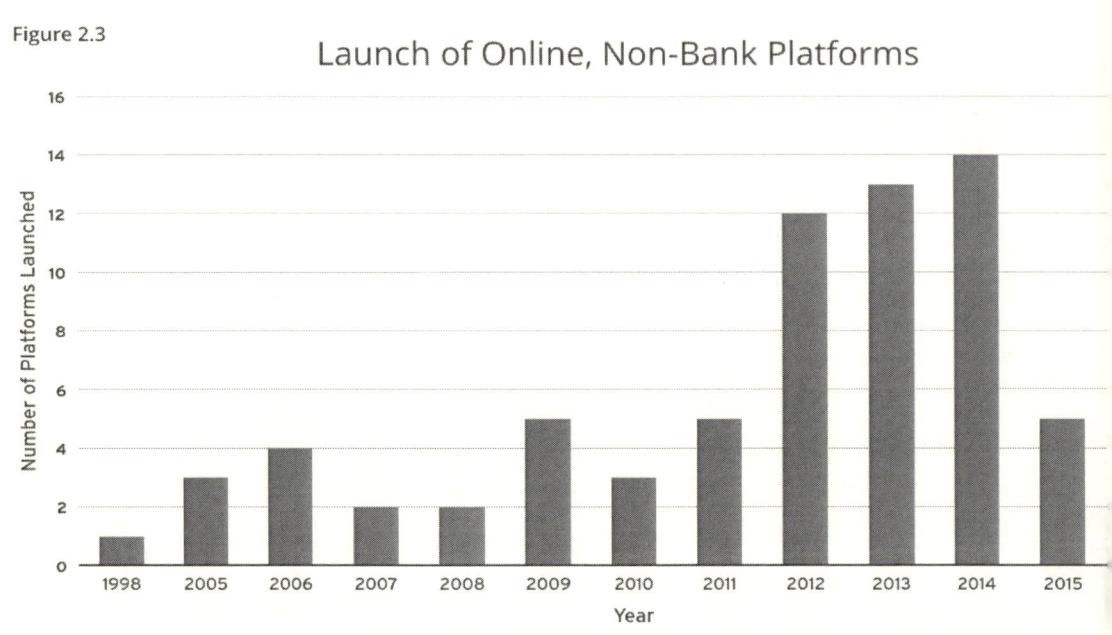

Figure 2.3

Launch of Online, Non-Bank Platforms

Year	Number of Platforms Launched
1998	1
2005	3
2006	4
2007	2
2008	2
2009	5
2010	3
2011	5
2012	12
2013	13
2014	14
2015	5

The U.S. Online, Non-Bank Finance Landscape; Milken Institute Center for Financial Markets - Jackson Mueller

The types of customers these new FinTech lenders serve varies by country. While accurate data on the size of the nonbank lending market is hard to come by, data collected by the Cambridge Center for Alternative Finance indicates that in the U.S., more than 80% of FinTech lending activity in 2015 was to the consumer sector, which includes student loans.[28]

This contrasts with lending activity by FinTechs in the United Kingdom – another FinTech hub – which is more evenly distributed across customer sectors. Over 40% of FinTech lending in the U.K is to businesses, while real estate accounts for over 20% of the FinTech lending market.

In China, the world's largest FinTech market, lending is near evenly split between consumers and businesses. While this data is a few years old, the approximate breakdown in FinTech lending by customer segment still holds true today. The reasons why this breakdown is so different across countries are numerous, but the biggest drivers are the strength of the traditional banking system and the regulatory regime in place in each country.

Figure 2.4 highlights some of the reasons why U.S. consumers borrow from FinTech lenders. This data comes again from Lending Club, one of the largest consumer FinTech lenders. It tracks over time the reason consumers give for their borrowing. The most common reason is for debt consolidation and this includes any type of non-credit card debt, such as student loan debt, debt incurred for medical expenses, or other kinds of unsecured debt. The second biggest reason consumers give for borrowing is to consolidate and pay off credit card debt. Credit cards tend to charge a very high rate of interest if you don't pay off your balance every month, so many consumers are turning to FinTech lenders to pay off this debt by obtaining a loan with a lower rate of interest.

Figure 2.4 Lending Club Loans (Origination Amount) by Loan Purposes by Origination Year 2007-2005

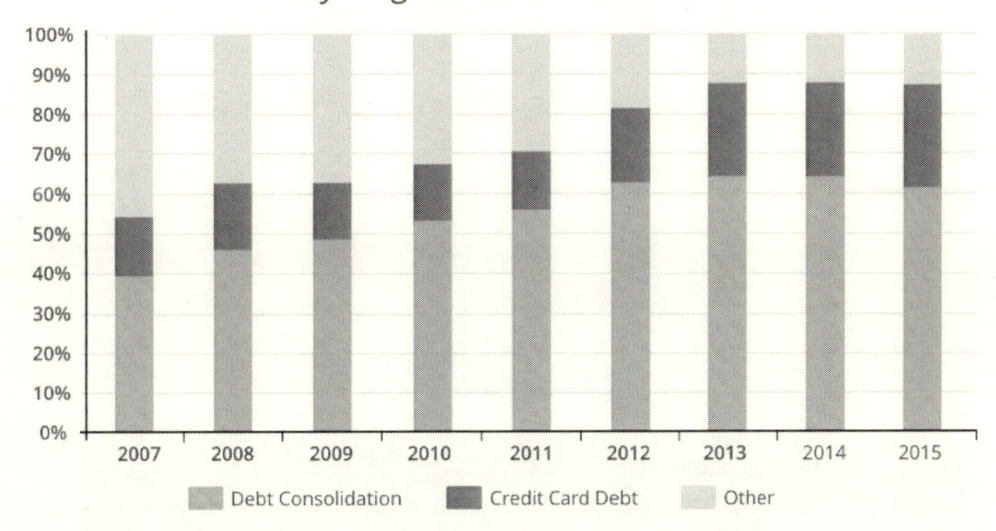

FinTech Lending: Financial Inclusion, Risk Pricing, and Alternative Information; Federal Reserve Bank of Philadelphia

China, the U.S., and the UK are three largest FinTech credit markets, with China being the largest market by far. In 2015, Chinese FinTech firms generated close to $100 billion dollars in new loans. In second place is the U.S., where $34 billion dollars in new FinTech loans were made in 2015. In third place is the United Kingdom, which generated around $4 billion in new FinTech loans in 2015. While the volume of FinTech credit generation in these countries is small compared to the volume of credit generated by traditional lenders, FinTech lending has still experienced astonishing growth. In 2013, Chinese FinTech firms originated $5.5 billion dollars in loans, meaning that in just two years, new FinTech loan volumes grew by close to 1,700%. The growth rate in the U.S.

was less dramatic but still impressive, with new loan growth going up by over 800% between 2013 and 2015.

In the United States, the FinTech lending market is highly concentrated, with the five largest platforms controlling around 80% of the market [see figure 2.5.] This may indicate there are limited profit opportunities for new entrants in the U.S.. The opposite is true in China, where over 350 FinTech credit platforms are all competing against each other and the top five platforms control no more than 25% of the market.

Figure 2.5

FinTech Credit Market Structure

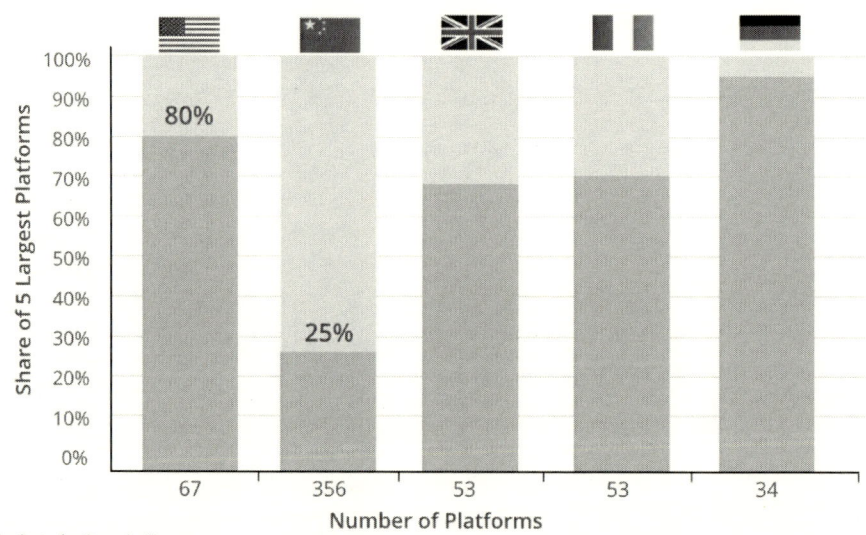

Share of 5 Largest Platforms

Number of Platforms	Share
67 (US)	80%
356 (China)	25%
53 (UK)	~68%
53	~70%
34	~95%

Data Source: Cambridge Center for Alternative Finance

Despite the rapid growth we've seen in FinTech credit markets, there's room to grow further because relatively few people have even heard of marketplace lending, or FinTech lending. In data that was included in a paper by the Federal Reserve Bank of Boston, only 25% of college graduates were aware of marketplace lending, and those without a college degree were even less likely to have ever heard of marketplace lending.[29] As consumers become more aware of the options available to them, they will increasingly turn to FinTech credit providers to meet their borrowing needs.

Regulatory and Legal Considerations

Regulatory and legal issues are driving business model decisions across the FinTech lending landscape. This is because nonbank FinTech lending platforms are regulated based on the activity they're engaged in. If a nonbank FinTech lending platform is engaged in loan underwriting, origination, or servicing, it will be subject to state-by-state lender licensing requirements, depending on the state that the lending platform is operating in. In addition, based on the activity of, and products provided by, the FinTech lending platform, they may be subject to federal or state consumer protection laws, federal or state securities laws, as well as federal anti-money laundering statutes. Also, consumer protection rules are the same for FinTech lenders as they are for any other credit intermediary, including banks.

FinTech lenders engaged in consumer lending are subject to numerous federal consumer protection laws. These include the Truth in Lending Act, the Home Ownership and Equity Protection Act, the Consumer Leasing Act, the Fair Debt Collection Practices Act, the Fair Credit Reporting Act, the Equal Credit Opportunity Act, the Credit Repair Organizations Act, the Electronic Funds Transfer Act, and the privacy provisions of the Gramm-Leach-Bliley Act. Nonbank FinTech lenders are subject to the statutory language included in all of these pieces of legislation and it's very important that FinTech lenders understand and internalize these obligations.

The Consumer Financial Protection Bureau (CFPB) is the agency responsible for enforcing the various federal consumer financial laws. In addition, the CFPB has supervisory authority over nonbank mortgage originators and servicers, payday lenders, and private student lenders of all sizes. So even if a FinTech lender is not a bank they can still be supervised by the CFPB, provided they meet certain conditions.

Nonbank lenders are also subject to state-by-state interest rate and fee restrictions that they can charge their customers. These are commonly referred to as usury laws. A loan is usurious if it charges an excessive rate of interest. Under the U.S. federal system, the regulation of usury is primarily left to the states. Each state addresses the issue by establishing a maximum interest rate that can be charged on loans that a state decides should be subject to the maximum rate cap. Federal law does not specify a federal usury rate, other than in very limited circumstances. It is important to note that there's a wide variation among the states as to the level of interest rate that constitutes "excessive." This is why you see many nonbank lenders, or even bank lenders, concentrated in specific states like Utah, who has no limit on the maximum legal interest rate.

These state-by-state interest rate restrictions don't apply to Federal Deposit Insurance Corporation (FDIC) insured banks, because federal banking law allows a bank insured by the FDIC to comply with the usury limits of its respective home state for all loans, including those loans that are made outside of the bank's home state. This means that an FDIC insured commercial bank or savings institution that engages in lending activities in more than one state is not burdened with the dilemma of addressing and resolving the differences in state-by-state usury laws because it only needs to observe the usury limits of the state where it is located. This outcome was confirmed in 1978, in a well-known U.S. Supreme Court decision: Marquette National Bank of Minneapolis v. First Omaha Service Corp.[30]

The exemption from state-by-state interest rate, or usury restrictions, is only available to banks. A nonbank FinTech lender that's offering loans to consumers in all 50 states will have to be licensed in each state and comply with each state's usury laws. This is why many FinTech credit platforms are partnering with banks, so that they can get around these state-by-state restrictions. They are able to do this by structuring their arrangements with banks in such a way that the FinTech credit platform markets to potential borrowers and negotiates, or assists negotiating, the loan agreement; and it's possible that they also may end up servicing and administering the loan. But the bank they're partnering will actually underwrite – or fund – the loan. This loan, once it's underwritten, may be sold back to the FinTech credit platform or to another intermediary a short time after it's originated. This whole process is configured to ensure that the bank is treated as the legal creditor. And because the bank is the legal creditor, the loan only needs to comply with the usury limit of the bank's home state. This structure enables the FinTech lending platform to avoid at least some state laws applicable to consumer lenders, including state licensing requirements. Just as importantly, this structure ensures that the bank is deemed the creditor for state usury purposes. This whole arrangement works because of the long-held legal principle known as Valid-When-Made, which simply means that a loan that is valid at its inception cannot subsequently become usurious upon transfer to another entity, even if that entity is not a bank.

Just because a nonbank FinTech lender partners with a bank to originate loans, does not mean that the FinTech lender escapes supervision by federal banking agencies. Banks of all sizes routinely rely on third-parties to provide critical services and to purchase loans originated by the bank. Because of this, a robust regime of third-party supervision has been established at the federal banking agencies to ensure that activities that occur outside of the bank are examined and supervised to the same extent as if they were being conducted by the bank itself. Bank sponsored lending programs with FinTech firms are no exception. The FDIC has published detailed guidance as to how these relationships should be managed and supervised.[31]

Common Lending Models

The business models highlighted in this section are stylized examples; the actual business model of any FinTech lender will likely differ in multiple ways. In fact, FinTech lenders may utilize multiple lending models in their business. Nonetheless, these stylized examples convey the basic structure of the FinTech lending industry.

We begin with the peer-to-peer lending model. The overarching idea behind peer-to-peer lending platforms is to have the platform provide an online market that allows lenders to trade directly with borrowers. The first step in this process is for a prospective borrower to apply for a loan on the platform. To help in this regard, borrowers will provide a range of credit information, which is then posted on the platform after it has been verified and approved. After the borrower applies for a loan, the next step is for prospective investors to choose which loans they want to fund, and to help investors make their decision, the FinTech platform will typically provide some sort of credit risk assessment, which will utilize their proprietary data algorithm.

In a pure matching model, investors will directly select prospective loans based on a range of credit information or specific criteria that they are looking for as an investor. These criteria could include the general loan purpose or the specific project being funded with the loan, the borrower's industry, the loan's term, or the borrower's income and other credit quality indicators. Once the investor decides they want to fund the loan, individual loan contracts are established between the borrower and the investor, rather than with the platform. As an alternative to individual loan contracts being established between investor and borrower, it is possible for the investment to take the form of shares in a pooled loan scheme. This is a common model in Japan where legislation does not allow retail creditors to lend directly to a borrower.

After the investor decides they want to fund specific loans, loan funds get dispersed directly to the borrower and then repayment of that loan is made directly to the lender/investor. None of those cash flows is done through the lending platform's own account. It's all connected through segregated accounts; the platform is simply operating as a middle man and earns revenue from fees levied on both the borrower and the investor.

The next FinTech lending model is known as the notary model, sometimes also referred to as the agency model. This model is fairly common in the United States. In the notary model, the FinTech platform offers a matching service similar to what they do in the peer-to-peer model, but the loan is originated by a partnering bank. In the U.S., some FinTech lenders partner with a bank so that they can use that institution's charter to make loans nationally, without having to obtain individual state licenses or having to comply with state by state interest rate restrictions.

In the notary model, the issuing depository institution originates loans to borrowers that apply on the online FinTech platform. After the loans are originated and subsequently held by the issuing depository institution for one or two days, they're purchased from the bank by the FinTech platform lender or by an investor through the platform lender. In a slight variation of this model, it is possible for the FinTech facilitated loans to be retained by the issuing bank and not be sold back to the FinTech platform or to other investors.

The platform lender may sell these loans to investors, who can be other banks, private funds or institutional investors. But these investors may not actually want to buy individual loans. So instead, they may buy payment dependent notes, which entitle them to a stream of payments directly linked to the performance of the loans. It is also possible for these loans to be securitized, in which case the issuing depository institution would sell the loans to a special purpose vehicle, which may be sponsored by the FinTech lending platform. That vehicle would then package groups of loans into asset backed securities and sell these securities to investors.

The final FinTech lending model worth mentioning is known as the balance sheet model. In this model, FinTech lending platforms originate and retain loans on their own balance sheet, akin to a traditional bank lender. The balance sheet model is more prominent in the United States than in other jurisdictions because the U.S. has deeper, more liquid financial markets. As the FinTech credit industry in the U.S. has developed, balance sheet lenders have increasingly relied on capital sources such as debt, equity and securitizations to fund their loan originations.

Just like the other models previously mentioned, under the balance sheet model, potential borrowers will go online and apply for a loan through the FinTech lending platform. The platform will conduct its credit risk analysis using its proprietary data algorithms. But in the balance sheet model, the loan is funded by the lending platform. So if the FinTech platform decides it wants to fund the loan, it will disperse the loan proceeds to the borrower and it'll keep that loan and hold it on its own balance sheet.

Balance sheet lenders require capital to fund their loans and they're able to get this capital from a variety of different sources in both debt and equity instruments. Venture capital funds, hedge funds, other banks, as well as other institutional investors may take an equity stake in the FinTech lender or purchase debt that is issued by the lending platform. The lending platform is then able to take the proceeds from this debt and equity to fund the loans that they retain on their balance sheets. Similar to the notary model, it is also possible for the lending platform to securitize the loans that they make.

It is worth briefly discussing U.S. securities law because the reality is that most investors don't want to own actual whole loans. There are multiple reasons for this, but essentially, the investor doesn't want to deal with the hassle of collecting on the debt if the loan borrower defaults. So instead of acquiring whole loans, most peer-to-peer and notary lenders issue some form of pass through note or pass through security to their funding source that is tied to the performance of the underlying loans. The U.S. Securities and Exchange Commission has determined that notes issued by peer-to-peer lenders to their funding sources are securities under federal securities law. Therefore, the FinTech lending platform needs to make sure that they're complying with applicable U.S. securities laws when they issue these pass through notes.

Table 2.1 classifies prominent FinTech lending platforms according to their stylized business model. The majority of FinTech lending platforms fall under the peer-to-peer lending model, where the platform is simply an intermediary that connects the borrower with the investor. The table also includes a column for the invoice trading, or factoring, model, which simply helps businesses manage their cash flow by allowing them to sell invoices or receivables to a third-party at a discount.

Table 2.1

Categorization of Prominent FinTech Lending

	Consumer	Business	Real Estate
Traditional/P2P	Funding Circle ThinCats LendInvest Assetz Capital Saving Stream	Funding Secure Zopa Lending Works Lendable	Wellesley LendInvest
Notary	LendingClub Auxmoney		
Balance Sheet	SoFi		Wellesley LendInvest

Data Source: Bank for International Settlements

FinTech lending firms can partner with banks in multiple ways. Banks can act as debt or equity investors or participate in securitization transactions with FinTech lenders. As equity investors, financial institutions can provide capital to FinTech lenders in exchange for equity. As debt investors, financial institutions can purchase whole loans to hold as assets.

Traditional lenders can also form distribution partnerships with FinTech lenders. To help serve borrowers better, a growing number of financial institutions have turned to FinTech lenders to offer new products or a more user-friendly experience. In referral partnerships, bank customers unable to meet certain underwriting criteria or seeking products not offered by their bank, are directed by the bank to a FinTech lender. These partnerships allow the bank to maintain customer relationships, while the FinTech lender is able to earn fee revenue on new loan originations. Under a co-branded or white label distribution partnership, financial institutions contract with FinTech lenders to integrate technology services into their product suite. Here, the FinTech lender provides its technological expertise to handle the entire loan process on either the FinTech lender's or the financial institution's website. Loans will then be originated by the financial institution, not by the FinTech lender, and reflect the underwriting standards of the financial institution.

Vulnerabilities of FinTech Credit

Because FinTech credit platforms exist entirely online and rely on relatively new digital processes, the first vulnerability worth highlighting is the potential for a major operational risk event, like a cyber-attack. Another vulnerability is the fact that new credit scoring algorithms developed by FinTech lenders are unproven. Most FinTech lenders came into existence after the 2008 financial crisis, a period in which markets have been steadily increasing. Eventually, the business cycle will turn, and at that point, some FinTech lenders may find out that their proprietary algorithm isn't as good or as accurate as they originally thought. If this happens, FinTech lenders may experience a wave of customer defaults and suffer large losses.

The FinTech lending business model also poses a threat to the health of the industry, through something that is known as moral hazard. Because most FinTech lenders end up selling the loans they make, they don't have a strong incentive to ensure that the borrower can pay back the loan. In fact, these lenders have an incentive to generate as many loans as possible because they earn fees on each loan issued. Given this fact, FinTech lenders may be willing to turn a blind eye to any borrower red flags because they don't want to miss out on their fee. If enough bad loans are issued, the entire industry could come crashing down during the next recession.

We saw a similar dynamic at play in the run up to the financial crisis, where many banks and nonbank mortgage originators engaged in what was known as an originate-to-distribute model, where they would make a mortgage loan and then sell the loan to someone else, who would then package the loan with many other mortgages and then sell securities that were tied to the performance of the underlying mortgages. Many of the mortgages underlying these mortgage backed securities were made to borrowers with extremely low credit scores or even to borrowers with no job or no income. Why? Because the entity making the loan was simply selling it on, and didn't bear any of the risk from a borrower default.

Another risk associated with the FinTech lending business model is the potential for investors to stop buying the loans being generated by the FinTech platform. Without investors willing to buy the loans, or notes tied to the performance of the loans, most FinTech lending platforms would be forced to shut down, or at least severally restrict the amount of new loans they issue. There are couple of reasons why investors may do this. The first is that a rise in interest rates could increase the return on other investable assets, thereby making the return associated with a portfolio of FinTech loans less attractive. To prevent investors from walking away, FinTech lending platforms may be forced to offer higher returns, which in turn would force them to charge a higher rate to borrowers. But if borrowers can obtain lower rates elsewhere, at a bank for instance, they may no longer be willing to borrow from FinTech lenders. Another risk is the loss in investor trust that would occur if FinTech lending platforms experienced higher rates of borrower defaults than what was otherwise expected by the platform and its investors. If this were to happen, investors may no longer deem the FinTech platform's credit risk models to be reliable, and therefore stop purchasing loans being generated by the FinTech lender. This risk could be exacerbated by poor transparency in respect of the underwriting process and loan performance. And of course, investor confidence could be shattered if any type of operational risk event were to happen, such as a cyber-attack, or some kind of internal fraud or operational disruption. An incident at lending club highlights this last point perfectly. Lending Club is one of the largest online lenders that emerged after the financial crisis. In 2016, it was revealed that Lending Club sold an investor $22 million in loans, whose characteristics violated the investor's express instructions. Lending Club's Board of Directors found that some people at the company knew the loans didn't meet the investor's criteria and that the application data on $3 million worth of these loans had been altered to make them comply.[32] These disclosures resulted in the resignation of the CEO and several other senior executives.

The FinTech lending industry is also vulnerable due to low barriers to entry. The industry is lightly regulated compared to banks, product distribution is online, and the data sources used are often widely available, all of which makes it relatively easy for new firms to set up shop. In addition to the threat from new entrants, FinTech lenders are also competing with traditional banks, many of whom have significant resources at their disposal and could set up their own platforms and make greater use of big data analytics and risk-based pricing. In fact, several large banks are already doing this.

FinTech lenders also face regulatory and legal risks. Nonbank FinTech lenders need to get licensed in every state in which they wish to do business, and there's a whole host of consumer protection laws they must adhere to. In addition, data-driven credit scoring algorithms carry the risk of disparate impact in credit outcomes and the potential for fair lending violations. Importantly, applicants do not have the opportunity to check and correct data potentially being used in underwriting decisions. While these rules and regulations may seem confusing and complicated to those with a technology background, failure to follow them could prove costly for FinTech lenders – or worse.

Finally, FinTech lenders may simply be unable to turn a profit. Eventually, platforms must be able to demonstrate that they can deliver sufficient returns to their shareholders, and most FinTech lending platforms have yet to do this. In 2017, OnDeck Capital lost over $12 million, and they have yet to turn a profit since they've gone public. In 2017, Lending Club lost $153 million, and they too have yet to turn a profit. While these FinTech platforms may be willing to suffer losses in the short-term in order to gain market share, their investor's patience is not unlimited. At some point, FinTech lenders will be forced to demonstrate they are capable of making money, and it is far from certain that they are.

Additional Legal Considerations

A recent court decision in the United States Court of Appeals for the Second Circuit has challenged the Valid-When-Made doctrine which underpins the relationship between FinTech credit providers and the banks they partner with. In this decision, in what's known as the Madden vs. Midland case, the Second Circuit found that a nonbank entity taking an assignment of debts originated by a national bank is not entitled to protection under the National Bank Act from state-law usury claims.[33]

The Valid-When-Made Doctrine means that a loan that is valid at its inception cannot subsequently become usurious or violate state interest rate restrictions upon subsequent transfer to another entity, even if that entity is not a bank. This Doctrine is a long-held legal principle that has been universally relied on in the lending business. If this principle is no longer valid, as a result of the Second Circuit decision, banks are severely limited in who they can sell their loans to, and the legal and commercial landscape for loan origination and sales activities will become, at the very least, materially less predictable.

The Second Circuit's decision has already had an impact on the FinTech lending industry in the states of New York, Connecticut, and Vermont. Some FinTech lenders have decided to exclude those states from their marketing and lending programs, or have decided to cap interest rates in those states in accordance with state usury limits. In securitization transactions, loans to borrowers in New York, Connecticut, and Vermont are sometimes excluded from the pools of loans to be purchased by the securitization vehicle, and a few FinTech lenders have decided to obtain state lending licenses instead of relying on national bank preemption, which allows them to partner with a bank who originates the loans and thereby get around the state-by-state interest rate restrictions.

Figure 2.6 highlights the impact the Madden decision has had on lending in the 2nd Circuit states of Connecticut, New York, and Vermont. It shows the growth in loan volume in the time period immediately after the original Madden decision, broken down by borrowers' credit score. For borrowers with the highest credit scores, the impact was minimal, with loan growth being roughly the same in the 2nd circuit as it was in other circuits. As you slide down the credit score scale, you begin to notice that post-Madden, loan growth in the second circuit was less than what it was in other circuits. In fact, for 2nd circuit borrowers with the worst credit scores, lending actually declined in the wake of the Madden decision, while it increased by over 100% everywhere else.

Figure 2.6

Growth in Loan Volume Post-Madden

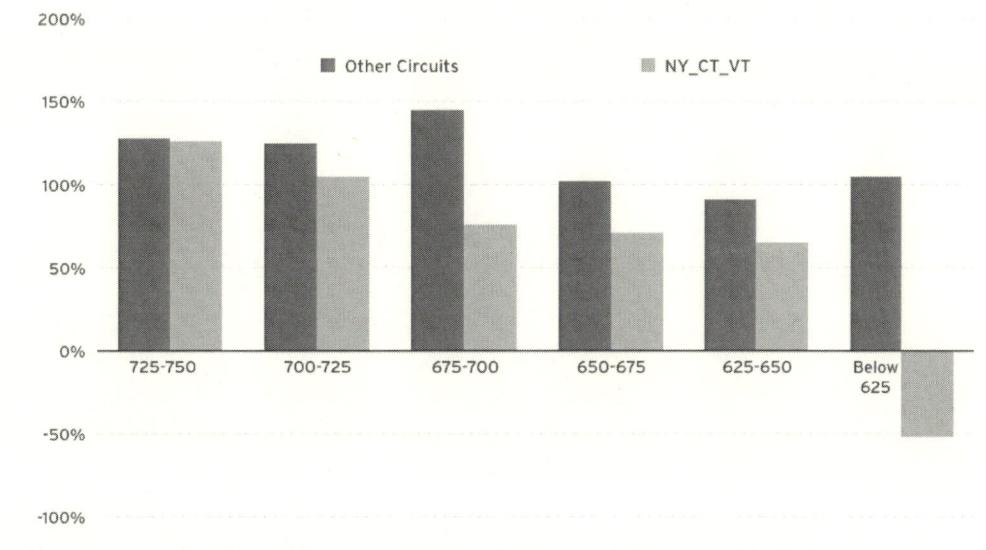

[Bar chart showing growth percentages by FICO score range for "Other Circuits" vs "NY_CT_VT":
- 725-750: Other Circuits ~130%, NY_CT_VT ~130%
- 700-725: Other Circuits ~125%, NY_CT_VT ~105%
- 675-700: Other Circuits ~145%, NY_CT_VT ~75%
- 650-675: Other Circuits ~100%, NY_CT_VT ~70%
- 625-650: Other Circuits ~90%, NY_CT_VT ~65%
- Below 625: Other Circuits ~105%, NY_CT_VT ~-60%]

What Happens when Loans Become Legally Void? Evidence from a Natural Experiment - Colleen Honigsberg, Robert J. Jackson Jr, Richard Squire

Some policymakers have expressed concern around the impact the Madden decision has had on consumer's access to credit and the overall uncertainty it has created in lending markets. New legislation has been introduced in Congress that would enshrine the Valid-When-Made principle into federal law.[34] However, that legislation is somewhat controversial and it's difficult to predict if it will ever become law.

Chapter 3: Banking Regulation in the United States

Creating and Regulating a Bank

While most FinTech lenders are nonbanks, many are starting to think seriously about becoming a bank due to the inherent advantages involved. The biggest advantage in being a bank is access to government insured deposits, which provide a cheap source of stable funding. Just think about how much you're earning on your checking or savings account and you'll understand why a FinTech company would be interested in funding their loans with deposits. Another advantage to being a bank is the ability to operate nationwide without having to get licensed in every state you wish to do business in or comply with each state's interest rate limits. There is also a potential competitive advantage if you're one of the first FinTechs to become a bank. Becoming a bank is difficult; FinTech companies who complete the rigorous process may be able to quickly grow market share over their competitors.

It is not easy to become a bank in the United States. This is because unlike most other companies, banks need permission from the government before they begin operating. Bill Gates and Paul Allen didn't need the government's permission when they started Microsoft in a tiny Albuquerque garage. Sam Walton didn't get the government's approval before he opened the first Walmart in Rogers Arkansas in 1962. So, what makes banks different? Banks are different because they play a unique and critical role in our economy, which brings with it intense government scrutiny.

The most important role banks play is that of custodian. Businesses and consumers alike place their hard-earned money at banks and trust that their bank will keep their money safe. When consumers lose trust in their bank, a bank run may occur, whereby a large number of a bank's customers withdraw their deposits simultaneously due to concerns that the bank may go out of business and take their money with it. Bank runs were a common site during the great depression but have since become less frequent due to the advent of government deposit insurance in 1933.

Banks are also unique because they allow the money supply to grow through what is known as fractional reserve banking. When I put a deposit into a bank, the bank is going to hold a certain portion of that as a reserve and then they will lend out the rest to a company or an individual who will in turn deposit some amount of the funds received into a bank, and the process repeats. Fractional reserve banking is critical for economic growth.

Banks also facilitate commerce through their role as intermediary. Savers of capital are able to safely place their funds at a bank who in turn lends those funds out to businesses and consumers who have a constructive use for this capital. This is a far more efficient process than me trying to lend my savings directly to other individuals or businesses.

Because banks play an essential role in our economy, if a bank, or series of banks, were to fail, it could potentially destabilize the entire financial system and negatively impact the rest of the economy. This is essentially what happened in 2008, when a decline in home prices led to many bank failures and the worst recession the United States has seen since the great depression.

Because of the critical role that banks play in our economy, and the potential consequences when banks fail, the government tightly controls who is allowed to become a bank and imposes regulations on existing banks that dictates what they can, and cannot, do. In the U.S., banks have to obtain a charter before they begin operating, which requires the sign-off of at least two regulatory agencies. The application process is rigorous and time consuming, taking a year or more. Extensive information about the organizer(s), the business plan, senior management team, finances, capital adequacy, risk management infrastructure, and other relevant factors must be provided to the appropriate authorities.

Figure 3.1 highlights the challenges associated with starting a new bank. In the wake of the financial crisis, new bank formation came to a standstill, with no new banks being created between 2009 and 2012. There are several reasons for this precipitous decline. First, regulators became much more cautious and risk-averse after the financial crisis. This has led them to more closely scrutinize new bank applications and impose more stringent regulations on exiting banks, both of which disincentivize new bank applications. Second, it has been a challenging business environment of late for smaller banks, with many struggling to cover their cost of capital. This makes it less attractive for those interested in starting a bank. More recently, regulatory agencies have taken steps to encourage new bank formation but their efforts have had little success. This is why many policymakers support the idea of allowing FinTech companies to become banks. Many believe it will promote healthy competition in the banking sector that will ultimately benefit consumers.

Figure 3.1

**Bank De Novo Applications Received
January 1, 2000 through June 30, 2016**

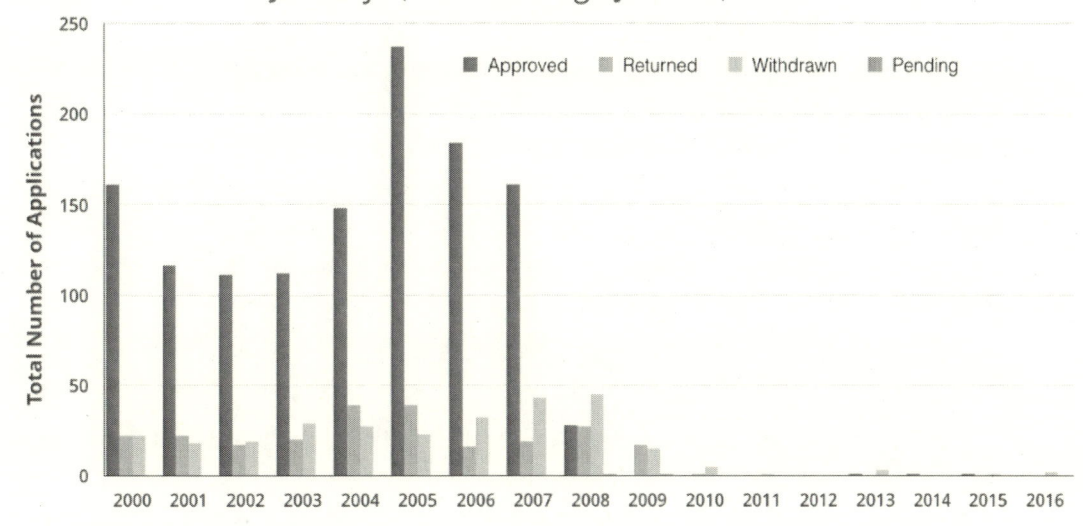

Data from FDIC on De Novo Banks and Industrial Loan Companies

There are multiple charters available to bank applicants. The most common type of charter, by far, is the commercial bank charter. Commercial banks offer your standard consumer and business banking services. Thrift charters are the next most common. Thrifts are much like commercial banks, except they are charged with a specific mission of promoting and bank rolling home ownership. Then there are credit unions. Credit unions are non-profit financial savings and lending cooperatives, whose members are also part owners. The next charter type worth mentioning is the industrial loan company charter, or ILC. ILCs are state chartered institutions that operate in seven states and have nearly all of the same powers as commercial banks. However, ILCs differ greatly from banks in that ILCs meeting certain conditions may be owned and operated by firms engaged in commercial activities, thus skirting the prohibitions on mixing banking and commerce that apply to virtually all other depository institutions. The ILC charter is an attractive option for many FinTech companies due to the limited federal oversight that comes with it. There are also charters for mutual savings banks, limited purpose trust companies and credit card banks.

Commercial bank charters, thrift charters and credit union charters can either be granted by the federal government or the states, and this concept is referred to as dual banking. For the most common form of bank charter, the commercial bank charter, the charter can either be granted at the federal level, by Office of the Comptroller of the Currency (OCC) or by the state banking agency in the applicant's home state. There is essentially no difference in the kinds of activities a state or federal chartered commercial bank can engage in.

Any commercial bank, either federally chartered or state chartered, is required to obtain Federal Deposit Insurance Corporation (FDIC) insurance. This means that the FDIC must also approve new bank charter applications. In addition, federally chartered banks (banks that are chartered by the OCC) are required to become a member of the Federal Reserve System. Think of the Federal Reserve system in this context, as simply a bank for other banks; the Federal Reserve system allows banks to place deposits at their local fed district bank, access the Federal Reserve payments system, and access emergency liquidity assistance that the Federal Reserve stands ready to provide to member banks in need. While state chartered banks must obtain FDIC insurance if they wish to accept customer deposits, they are not required to become members of the Federal Reserve System, although they may do so if they wish.

The majority of both nationally and state chartered banks are wholly owned by holding companies, and these holding companies are referred to as bank holding companies because they own a banking subsidiary. The Federal Reserve Board is the agency responsible for regulating bank holding companies while the banking subsidiary that sits underneath the holding company is supervised by either the OCC or the relevant state banking authority. In its role as bank holding company regulator, the Federal Reserve will supervise all activity that occurs within and underneath the holding company, including activity in the bank and nonbank subsidiaries.

Many financial entities prefer the holding company structure because it gives them greater flexibility into the types of activities they can engage in. In addition, holding companies have greater flexibility when it comes to buying back their stock, which is something that shareholders are typically supportive of.

Figure 3.2 provides more perspective on the predominant types of bank charters by displaying the share of FDIC insured deposits held by charter class. Over 60% of deposits are held at nationally chartered commercial banks. Following behind that, 16% of deposits are held by state chartered commercial banks who choose to be members of the Federal Reserve System and 15% of deposits are held by state chartered commercial banks that are not members of the Federal Reserve System. Figure 3.2 demonstrates that the vast majority of deposits in the banking system are held by state and nationally chartered commercial banks.[2]

---

[2] Note that credit unions are not listed on this chart because their deposits are insured by the National Credit Union Administration, not the FDIC.

Figure 3.2

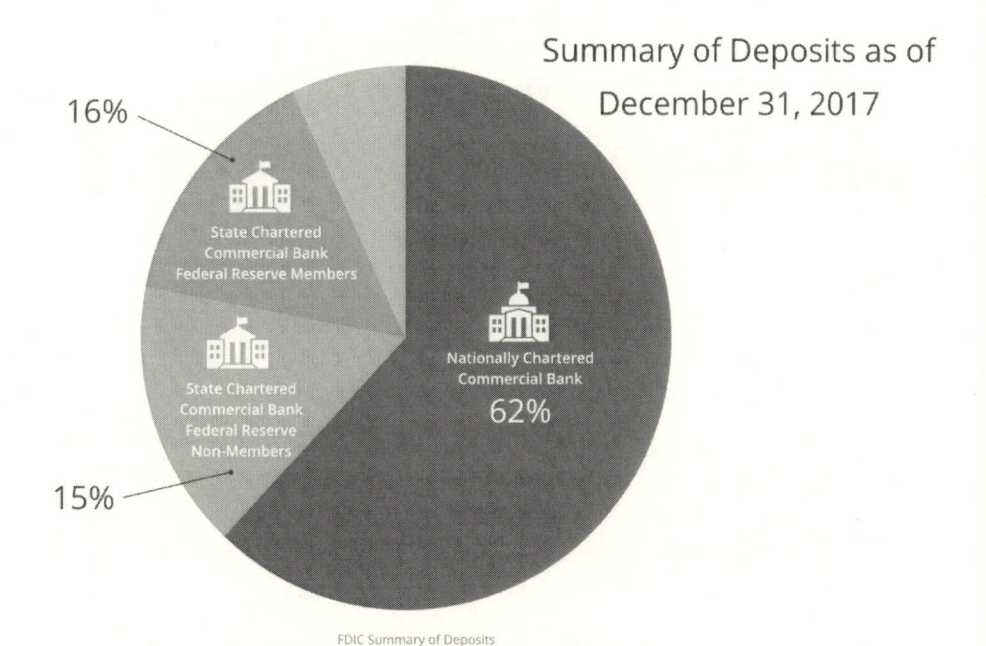

Summary of Deposits as of December 31, 2017

- 16% — State Chartered Commercial Bank Federal Reserve Members
- 15% — State Chartered Commercial Bank Federal Reserve Non-Members
- 62% — Nationally Chartered Commercial Bank

FDIC Summary of Deposits

Understanding the jurisdiction of the various regulatory agencies responsible for regulating banks in the U.S. can be confusing – even for those within the financial industry. The first thing you need to know is that most banks are regulated by at least two agencies. This will include the bank's prudential regulator, who is focused on ensuring the bank is operating in a safe and sound manner, and another agency who may have a more narrow focus.

The FDIC will have supervisory authority over any institution that accepts customer deposits – outside of credit unions – regardless of if it is state or federally chartered. The OCC is the primary regulator for all nationally chartered banks while the applicable state agency will be the primary regulator for state chartered banks. Because all nationally chartered banks are required to become members of the Federal Reserve System, the Federal Reserve will also supervise national banks as well as state charted banks that chose to become members of the Federal Reserve System. The Federal Reserve is also the primary regulator for all bank holding companies and savings and loan holding companies. And finally, the Consumer Financial Protection Bureau, which was created after the financial crisis, has supervisory authority over banks, thrifts, and credit unions with assets over $10 billion dollars as well as their affiliates. This information can be confusing, but when it comes to FinTech, it is important to know because it highlights that there is no single government agency that has sole discretion over whether or not a FinTech company can become a bank.

Special Purpose FinTech Charter

In 2016, recognizing that the bank regulatory framework was unfamiliar to nonbank FinTech companies who either wished to partner with banks or become a bank themselves, the Office of the Comptroller of the Currency (OCC) released its Responsible Innovation Framework, which, among other things, established an Office of Innovation to serve as a central point of contact for FinTech companies seeking guidance on regulatory matters.[35] To help facilitate communication between FinTech firms and the OCC, the agency set up new offices in the FinTech hubs of New York and San Francisco where they meet frequently with FinTech firms who are seeking guidance or clarification on regulations that may apply to their business. The Responsible Innovation Framework also mentioned the possibility of an OCC pilot program that would, "Facilitate adoption of new solutions and enhancement of risk management by permitting testing and discovery before full scale commitment and roll out." This concept is similar to the regulatory sandboxes that have been deployed in other countries. However, the OCC has yet to follow through on this sandbox concept and it is uncertain if they ever will.

Several months after rolling out their responsible innovation framework, the OCC announced that they would be moving forward with a proposal to charter FinTech companies that offer products and services similar to what banks offer and that meet the agencies standards and chartering requirements. In their proposal, the OCC listed several reasons why they believe a FinTech charter would benefit the public. First, applying a bank regulatory framework to FinTech companies would help ensure that these companies operate in a safe and sound manner so that they can effectively serve the needs of customers, businesses and communities. Second, applying the OCC's uniform supervision over national banks, including FinTech companies, will help promote consistency in the application of law and regulation across the country and ensure that consumers are treated fairly. And finally, providing a path for FinTech companies to become national banks can make the federal banking system stronger. The OCC's oversight not only would help ensure that these companies operate in a safe and sound manner, it would also encourage them to explore new ways to promote fair access and financial inclusion and innovate responsibly.

It is clear that the OCC's decision to propose a FinTech bank charter is largely driven by the agency's belief that FinTech innovations hold the potential to better serve customers who have historically been left out of the banking system. In a December 2016 speech announcing the FinTech charter proposal, the then Comptroller of the Currency Thomas Curry said: "What excites me most about the changes occurring in financial services is the great potential to expand financial inclusion, reach unbanked and underserved populations, make products and services faster, safer and more efficient and accelerate their delivery."[36]

The OCC's announcement was met by skepticism from those who claim the agency does not have the legal authority to issue a new bank charter specifically for FinTech companies. The OCC argues that they do have this authority because the National Bank Act grants them the ability, among other things, to charter what are known as Special Purpose National Banks. Historically, the most common types of special purpose national banks have been trust banks, which are national banks limited to the activities of a trust company, and credit card banks, which are national banks limited to a credit card business. However, the OCC believes that there is no legal limitation on the type of "special purpose" for which a national bank charter may be granted, provided the entity is engaged in what's referred to as the "business of banking."

Historically, the OCC has interpreted the business of banking to be any activity that is related to receiving deposits, paying checks, or lending money, and the courts have largely upheld this classification. This definition is also broad enough to have allowed the OCC to deem previous technological developments as falling under the business of banking. Therefore, the OCC believes that provided a FinTech company is providing any kind of product or service that is related to receiving deposits, paying checks, or lending money, they have the authority to issue a special purpose national bank charter to the company.

The biggest advantage in obtaining a national bank charter for a FinTech firm is the ability to conduct business on a nationwide basis and preempt most state banking regulations. However, a FinTech charter does not allow the recipient to circumvent all state banking laws. There are some state laws that apply to all nationally chartered banks, including laws on anti-discrimination, fair lending, and debt collection. In addition, many federal statutes are based on the type of financial activity a company is engaged in, regardless of whether or not they hold a bank charter. For instance, any entity engaged in consumer lending must comply with the truth in lending act and any entity making consumer real-estate loans must comply with the Real Estate Settlement Procedures Act and the Home Mortgage Disclosure Act.[3]

There are other federal statutes that apply only to FDIC-insured depository institutions. This includes the Community Reinvestment Act, which was designed to encourage commercial banks and savings associations to help meet the needs of borrowers in segments of their community, including low and moderate-income neighborhoods. Thus, if a FinTech receives the special purpose national bank charter but does not hold deposits, they will not be subject to the Community Reinvestment Act.

If a FinTech were to receive a special purpose national bank charter, they would be subject to the same regulations, examination, reporting requirements, and ongoing supervision as other national banks. In fact, the OCC has made it clear that statutes that

---

[3] Please note that this is not an exhaustive list of applicable lending laws, rather, I am just highlighting the point that many federal statutes apply to banks and nonbanks alike.

by their terms apply to national banks apply to all special purpose national banks, even uninsured national banks.

As part of the FinTech charter proposal, the OCC noted that the same application process that applies to all national banks will also apply to FinTech charter applicants. The agency also listed their baseline expectations that they expect any FinTech company seeking a national bank charter to meet.[37] These include expectations that the company have a detailed business plan and a robust governance and compliance framework. The company needs to hold sufficient amounts of capital to stay solvent at all times and have a plan for how they will accomplish this. They also need to maintain a ready amount of liquid assets that they can monetize if they ever come under stress. Finally, the OCC expects FinTech charter applicants to have a plan for how they will serve the financial needs of all members of the community they operate in as well as a plan for how the company can be wound down if they ever get into severe distress, otherwise known as a recovery and resolution plan.

These are not easy requirements to meet; it can be especially challenging for FinTech companies who are more tech focused and have limited experience in the financial services industry and are therefore not accustomed to dealing with financial regulators. As such, many FinTech companies feel that the application process is too onerous and that the benefits of obtaining a special purpose national bank charter may not outweigh the costs, which includes ongoing, rigorous, OCC supervision.

The OCC has yet to offer special purpose FinTech charters due to ongoing legal challenges. However, even if the agency stood ready to grant the charter, it may not prove meaningful unless other regulators were willing to cooperate. Recall that all national banks are required to become members of the Federal Reserve System and comply with applicable Federal Reserve rules and regulations. Presumably, the Federal Reserve would allow a FinTech company that receives a special purpose national bank charter to become a Federal Reserve member, but they have been silent on the question so far. Also remember that the Federal Reserve supervises bank holding companies, so if a FinTech charter recipient was owned by a holding company, the Federal Reserve would have the authority to supervise the holding company and all the subsidiaries controlled by the holding company. To make this concept more concrete, imagine that Amazon sets up a new subsidiary that makes loans to Amazon customers and this subsidiary applies for, and receives, the OCC's special purpose national bank charter. This would then mean that the OCC would supervise Amazon's banking subsidiary while the Federal Reserve would supervise Amazon's holding company and all the subsidiaries underneath of it. Essentially, this gives the Federal Reserve the right to look into everything Amazon does, even if it's not related to banking.

Recall how one of the benefits of being a bank is access to customer deposits, which provide a cheap source of funding. Any bank seeking to hold customer deposits must get approval from the FDIC. Thus far, the FDIC has not indicated how they would view an application for deposit insurance if it was coming from a FinTech company that received the OCC's special purpose national bank charter.

The OCC's FinTech charter has been controversial from the beginning. Many states expressed concern that payday lenders would use the FinTech charter has an end-around state laws that prohibit, or severally curtail, payday lending in their state. Others are worried that the FinTech charter could allow large commercial entities like Google or Facebook to get into the banking industry, thereby eroding the separation of banking and commerce. And yet others are concerned that virtual currency businesses could receive a Special Purpose FinTech Charter and therefore preempt state laws that apply to virtual currency businesses.

Reflecting these concerns, the Conference of State Bank Supervisors and the New York Department of Financial Services sued the OCC, arguing that the agency does not have the authority to issue charters to firms that do not engage in deposit taking and other traditional banking activities. The New York Department of Financial Services lawsuit was thrown out because the judge ruled that the case was speculative due to the OCC having yet to finalize their plans for the Charter.[38]

Thus far, no court has weighed in on whether or not the OCC has the authority to charter FinTech companies. The current Comptroller of the Currency, Joseph Otting, expects to take a final position on the proposed FinTech charter relatively soon. In fact, by the time you read this book, the OCC may have made their decision. Regardless of what happens with the FinTech charter, there are other options available to FinTech companies seeking to become a bank and access customer deposits.

Industrial Loan Company Charter

Rather than wait around in the hopes that the OCC will one day accept FinTech charter applications, several FinTechs who are interested in becoming a bank are pursuing other alternatives. The principal alternative is the Industrial Loan Company, or ILC, charter, which is a type of charter that gives non-financial institutions the ability to enter the banking industry without being subject to the same level of supervisory oversight that applies to commercial banks. Industrial loan companies emerged in the early 1900s as small niche lenders that provided consumer credit to low and moderate-income workers who were generally unable to obtain consumer loans from commercial banks.[39] ILCs have changed dramatically in size and structure since these early days. Thirty years ago, there were around 120 ILCs open for business, and industry assets totaled $7.5 billion. Today, there are only 25 ILCS in existence and industry assets exceed $180 billion.

ILCs are state chartered, with only a handful of states authorizing them, Utah being the most prominent among them due to their low corporate tax rate, virtually non-existent usury caps, and friendly regulatory environment. ILCs have virtually all of the same powers and privileges as insured commercial banks, including the protections of the federal safety net, such as deposit insurance and access to the Federal Reserve's discount window and payments system. Many ILCs even use the word bank in their name, including: Toyota Financial Savings Bank, WebBank, and BMW Bank of North America. The key difference between ILCs and commercial banks is that ILCs operate under a special exception to the Federal Bank Holding Company Act, which means they are not subject to the same Federal Reserve prudential supervision as applies to bank holding companies and are therefore not required to maintain the separation of banking and commerce which congress has historically mandated for bank holding companies. Policymakers from both parties have largely supported this separation, due to concerns that if allowed to control a bank, commercial entities would simply use it to provide subsidized funding to their nonbank subsidiaries, thereby creating an uneven playing field for those commercial firms that do not own a bank. In addition, because banks receive FDIC deposit insurance which lowers their overall cost of funding, taxpayers would in effect be subsidizing the operations of the commercial entity.

The ILC charter is an attractive option for some FinTech firms who are looking to become a bank and gain access to consumer deposits because the corporate owners of an ILC are not subject to consolidated supervision by the Federal Reserve. Harley-Davidson, Toyota, and Target all own ILCs, but unlike bank holding companies, these companies do not have the Federal Reserve, or any other federal banking agency, looking into all of their activities. Rather, the FDIC and relevant state banking agency will supervise and examine the ILC subsidiary in isolation. It is easy to understand why a technology company with a FinTech subsidiary would not want the Federal Reserve sniffing around all aspects of their business.

As you might imagine, the ILC charter is controversial. In 2005, Walmart applied for a Utah industrial loan company charter, which engendered intense public outrage.[40] In response, the FDIC enacted a moratorium on new ILC charters, and in 2010 the Dodd-Frank Act required a temporary moratorium on ILC charters which expired in 2013. The FDIC has yet to approve an ILC application since the temporary moratorium expired. But several FinTech firms are hoping that the FDIC will change their stance on ILC applications. In June of 2017, online lender SoFi applied for a Utah-based ILC charter that would allow them to open a full-service online only bank.[41] SoFi ended up withdrawing their application several months later after a series of scandals tarnished the company's reputation.[42] In September 2017, the payments processor Square also applied for a Utah-based ILC charter.[43] Square has been slowly branching out into providing small business loans and an ILC charter would allow the company to fund these loans with deposits. Square withdrew their ILC application in July of 2018 but the company plans on refiling at a later date after they strengthen some areas of their FDIC application.[44] If the FDIC were to approve Square's application, it would likely usher in a wave of new ILC applications from FinTech firms eager to gain access to deposits. Beyond the OCC's FinTech charter and the ILC charter, another option available to FinTech firms eager to become a bank, is to apply for a standard national bank charter. This is what mobile-only financial institution Varo Money did in July of 2017.[45] There is no requirement that a national bank have brick and mortar branches, and Varo is hopeful that their application will be approved by the OCC and FDIC. While the path FinTech companies must take to become a bank remains uncertain, the desire to access cheap customer deposits and freely operate nationwide is not going away. Expect more FinTech companies to apply for some form of bank charter in the years ahead.

Chapter 4: Cryptocurrency and Initial Coin Offerings

Explaining Cryptocurrency

The legal and regulatory environment surrounding cryptocurrencies and initial coin offerings (ICOs) is complex, uncertain, and changing by the day. While I could not possibly summarize every law and regulation that applies to cryptocurrencies and ICOs in this chapter, I do hope to impart to you an understanding of the key issues that any business operating in this space must consider. Failing to understand and consult applicable rules and regulations could prove fatal to any cryptocurrency business.

To understand the legal and regulatory issues surrounding cryptocurrencies, you must first understand how cryptocurrencies work at a high level. Most cryptocurrencies use some form of distributed ledger, which is a database that is spread across several nodes or computing devices. Each node replicates and saves an identical copy of the ledger. Each participant node on the network updates itself independently and the ledger is not maintained by any central authority.

The most prominent form of distributed ledger technology is blockchain, which powers the well-known cryptocurrency Bitcoin. But blockchain is also used to enable a number of public and private virtual currencies, as well as other applications. The Bitcoin blockchain is an immutable record of every single transaction that ever occurred in the Bitcoin network. Often referred to as a public ledger, blockchain is a log that contains metadata about when and how each transaction occurred. The ledger is publicly accessible, and to prevent tampering with current and past transactions, the database is cryptographically secured. Encryption allows developers to trust the transaction history and build applications from and around transaction information.

Blockchain can be both public and private; so in a public blockchain like the Bitcoin blockchain, anyone has access to it. It is available universally and you don't need permission to become a node and see all the transactions that occur on the Bitcoin blockchain. It is also possible for a blockchain to be private, or permissioned, where access is controlled; and this is the type of blockchain that is being increasingly deployed in the financial services industry as well as other sectors because certain business segments do not want everyone to be able to access the distributed database.

Blockchain powers the Bitcoin software and the decentralized computer network of users running that software. The Bitcoin software and protocols were first described in a white paper released in 2008 by an author using the penname Satoshi Nakamoto; and Bitcoin itself was released in a proof-of-concept software client in January 2009. The Bitcoin community progressively built out a decentralized network of computers that exert a tremendous amount of computing power toward the singular purpose of validating and clearing transactions on the Bitcoin network. The distributed and decentralized network allows each individual user to verify the validity of individual transactions and the system as a whole, through the cryptographic protocols and the transaction history of the Bitcoin network, which is stored by each user on the blockchain. Information or transactions are added to the blockchain through the proof-of-work mining process. Users running a special mining variant of the Bitcoin software expend a great amount of computing power in order to win the right to add another block to the blockchain, which is accompanied by a reward of Bitcoins. The concept of proof-of-work mining ensures an adjusted amount of work and computing power must be expended to solve a block, with a block reward of a certain amount of Bitcoin providing an economic incentive for honest mining. The expenditure of computing power serves to secure the integrity of the blockchain; while the miners themselves verify through public-key cryptography the validity of each transaction they include in a block. When a transaction is included in a block, the transaction has been validated and cleared by the miner.

Bitcoin is different from traditional fiat – or government sponsored – currency in a variety of ways. The first is that it is decentralized, meaning there is no central authority controlling the currency's issuance. The second difference is that accessing the Bitcoin network is relatively easy. Anyone with a laptop or computer can become a node on the Bitcoin network and begin sending transactions through it. Bitcoin is also 'pseudo-anonymous,' meaning that your personal information is not identifiable on the Bitcoin network. Instead, users are only referred to by their public key – or address – a long string of alpha-numeric characters. Bitcoin is not fully anonymous because every transaction ever conducted by a single address is stored forever in the blockchain. If your address is ever linked to your identity, every transaction will be linked to you. Bitcoin is also unique because it is completely transparent; every transaction in the history of the Bitcoin network is available to all nodes on the network. And finally, unlike most non-cash transactions, Bitcoin transactions are irreversible; once a Bitcoin is sent to another node on the network, there is no way for that transaction to be reversed, unless the node who received the original Bitcoin is willing to send it back.

While Bitcoin today is a widely known and utilized cryptocurrency, it did not get to this point without experiencing some significant growing pains. The first high profile case was the online black market known as Silk Road. Silk Road was a marketplace for selling illegal drugs and other illicit goods that operated on the dark web and utilized Bitcoin as its preferred method of payment because of the pseudo anonymity it provides. In October 2013, the FBI shut the website down and arrested its founder for omnibus violations of federal drug and anti-money laundering laws.[46] He was sentenced to a lengthy prison term and ordered to pay restitution of $183 million dollars; representing all sales of illegal items on Silk Road.

2013 is also when the price of Bitcoin began to increase, climbing from $13 at the start of the year to nearly $1,000 at its peak towards the end of the year. At the time, online exchange Mt. Gox handled 70% of the world's Bitcoin trades. Beginning in April, Mt. Gox started experiencing technical difficulties and had to suspend trading for a few days for what they called a "market cool down." By November of 2013, Mt. Gox customers were experiencing delays of weeks to months in withdrawing funds from their accounts and cashing out had become difficult to impossible. Finally, in February of 2014, Mt. Gox halted all withdrawals, and less than 2 weeks later it suspended trading, closed its website and exchange service, and filed for a form of bankruptcy protection under Japanese law to allow courts to seek a buyer. Mt. Gox then announced that around 850 thousand of their customer's Bitcoins, valued at roughly $480 million dollars at the time, were missing and had likely been stolen.[47] This checkered past makes Bitcoin's, and other cryptocurrencies, subsequent price increases and mass adoption all the more remarkable.

The problem's highlighted by Silk Road and Mt. Gox have not gone away. Cryptocurrencies are still used to facilitate illegal transactions and ransomware hackers frequently demand payment in Bitcoin. Cryptocurrency exchanges are also still vulnerable to hacks. In January 2018, Japanese exchange CoinCheck surpassed Mt. Gox as target of the largest cryptocurrency theft in history when hackers stole over $530 million dollars of the cryptocurrency NEM from users' accounts.[48]

Despite these obvious perils, Bitcoin has experienced a meteoric rise the past couple of years, as shown in Figure 4.1. In addition, the growth in Bitcoin ushered in an explosion of new digital currencies. Currently there are over 1,800 unique cryptocurrencies.[49]

Figure 4.1

Price of Bitcoin

Data Source: Coindesk Bitcoin pricing

What is driving this apparently insatiable demand for cryptocurrency? The answer is not entirely clear, but there are a several contributing factors that are worth mentioning. The first is the ease with which you can now acquire cryptocurrency. In the early days of Bitcoin, buying and selling the cryptocurrency required a fairly high degree of technological sophistication. But now, if you live in a major metropolitan area, chances are you can walk to a nearby Bitcoin ATM where all you have to do is download a free digital coin wallet, insert the desired amount of cash, place your phone up to the scanner and – voila! –you own Bitcoin.[50] In addition, consumers have access to dozens of online exchanges that make buying and selling cryptocurrencies pretty easy. Increased technological familiarity along with network effects have also been factors fueling the demand for cryptocurrencies. There are now many online resources that are designed to teach people about cryptocurrencies as well as popular Bitcoin related documentaries on platforms like Netflix. As more and more consumers become aware of cryptocurrencies through these channels as well as through an influx of news stories, network effects start to kick-in. The network effect describes the phenomenon whereby a technology or innovation becomes more valuable simply because more people are using it. It is certainly the case that the more people are familiar with, and willing to accept cryptocurrencies as payment, the more valuable cryptocurrencies become.

Another factor that is driving market demand for the most popular cryptocurrencies (like Bitcoin and Ether) is the red-hot initial coin offering market, where a company issues digital coins or tokens that provide access to a service (often called a "utility" or "app" token) or that represent an investment opportunity in the company (like a traditional security). Purchasing these digital tokens typically requires the buyer to remit either Bitcoin or Ether, which therefore increases the demand for these cryptocurrencies.

Another demand factor that has been suggested is a continuing post-financial crisis distrust of the traditional banking sector and governmental institutions. Traditional currencies are typically issued and controlled by a country's central bank and payments utilizing these currencies must go through bank intermediaries, but cryptocurrencies are not controlled by one central authority and can be sent from one user to another, without having to go through any kind of intermediary. In addition, most cryptocurrencies set a cap on the total amount that can ever be circulated, thereby preventing their value from being inflated away. Along these lines, political instability in countries like Venezuela, Zimbabwe and Syria has created demand for cryptocurrencies. These countries have seen bouts of hyperinflation, which has eroded the purchasing power of the official currency. Bitcoin has become an attractive option for consumers in these countries because it lies outside the government's control and is considered to have a more stable value.

Another reason for the run up in the price of cryptocurrencies, particularly Bitcoin, is its ability to facilitate criminal activity and to make transactions anonymously – away from the informational reach of governments and regulators. Many of these transactions are explicitly illegal (like money laundering) while others are controversial, like donating to WikiLeaks. In addition to fueling illicit activity, cryptocurrencies can also be involved in more traditional securities market fraud, like pump and dump and Ponzi schemes. While cryptocurrencies are clearly used for nefarious purposes, it is difficult to determine exactly how much this activity contributes to the price. Cryptocurrency (in particular Bitcoin) does remain, for the moment, the criminal currency of choice for hackers because of its anonymity and the ability to convert it into cash (or "wash" it) in the "dark net."[51]

The final, and most important reason for the extraordinary rise in cryptocurrencies is simply human psychology. Over the past several years, consumers have been fed a steady stream of news headlines about individuals striking it rich by investing in cryptocurrencies. As a case in point, consider the following headlines from the Telegraph and Forbes respectively: "Idaho teenager becomes millionaire by investing $1,000 gift in Bitcoin–and wins bet with his parents"[52] and "Meet the Man Traveling the World On $25 Million Of Bitcoin Profits."[53] These stories entice more people to invest in cryptocurrencies, which pushes prices even higher. Thus, it appears that many people invest in cryptocurrencies simply because they think they will be able to sell for a higher price in the future.

This observation has led many people to call the cryptocurrency market a massive bubble that will soon pop. In fact, the cryptocurrency market – particularly Bitcoin – did cool off after reaching peak hysteria in December of 2017. On December 17, 2017, the price of one Bitcoin reached an all-time high of $19,511, which coincided with the day Bitcoin futures started trading on the Chicago Mercantile Exchange (CME).[54] As of July 11th, 2018, the price was close to $6,300 and volatility in the Bitcoin market had come down from levels seen in 2017. Regardless of what happens to their price, cryptocurrencies are here to stay.

Regulating Cryptocurrency as Money

There is no one agency that has exclusive jurisdiction over cryptocurrencies and different agencies have different interpretations of what cryptocurrency is that largely reflect each agency's statutory mandate. Cryptocurrency first came under the regulatory umbrella as a form of money. The Financial Crimes Enforcement Network (FinCEN) is a bureau of the United States Department of the Treasury that collects and analyzes information about financial transactions in order to combat domestic and international money laundering, terrorist financing, and other financial crimes. FinCEN is responsible for enforcing the Bank Secrecy Act, the nation's first and most comprehensive Federal anti-money laundering and counter-terrorism financing statute. In 2011 and again in 2013, FinCEN issued guidance clarifying the applicability of the regulations implementing the Bank Secrecy Act to persons creating, obtaining, distributing, exchanging, accepting, or transmitting virtual currencies.[55][56] The guidance states that "administrators and exchangers," of convertible virtual currencies are subject to FinCEN regulations governing money transmitters; while users of virtual currencies are exempt. A user is a person that obtains virtual currency to purchase goods or services. An exchanger is a person engaged as a business in the exchange of virtual currency for real currency funds or other virtual currency. An administrator is a person engaged as a business in issuing or putting into circulation a virtual currency, and who has the authority to redeem such virtual currency. Note that in this context, a person can be an actual human being or a company.

FinCEN's guidance makes clear that the definition of a money transmitter does not differentiate between real currencies and convertible virtual currencies. Accepting and transmitting anything of value that substitutes for currency makes a person a money transmitter under the regulations implementing the Bank Secrecy Act. Therefore, any individual or company operating in the cryptocurrency space, other than those persons who obtain cryptocurrency to buy goods or services, is most likely subject to FinCEN regulations governing money transmitters and must comply accordingly.

Ripple, a well-known payments and cryptocurrency company, provides an example of what can happen when firms fail to comply with FinCEN regulations. In 2015, FinCEN assessed a $700,000-dollar civil money penalty against Ripple for willfully violating several requirements of the Bank Secrecy Act by acting as a money services business and selling its virtual currency, known as XRP, without registering with FinCEN, and by failing to implement and maintain an adequate anti-money laundering program designed to protect its products from use by money launderers or terrorist financiers.[57] In the press release announcing the penalty, the Department of Justice sent a clear message to all cryptocurrency firms by stating: "Ripple Labs Inc. and its wholly-owned subsidiary both have acknowledged that digital currency providers have an obligation not only to refrain from illegal activity, but also to ensure they are not profiting by creating products that allow would–be criminals to avoid detection. We hope that this sets an industry standard in the important new space of digital currency."[58]

The act of transferring money or value from one person to another also brings into play the state statutes licensing money transmitters. State licensing requirements vary from state to state, but typically include some form of minimum net worth, maintenance of a bond, annual audits, examinations by regulators, record-keeping, anti-money laundering programs, and a list of permissible investments for funds received and held. State money transmission statutes are clearly triggered when a money transmitter maintains an office or an agent in a state, but a physical presence is not necessary to invoke the statute and merely having an internet website that does not block access to a resident in a state may be enough to implicate a state's licensing requirements.

Since state money transmission statutes typically apply to the transmission of "money" or "funds," the key question then becomes: do cryptocurrencies qualify as money or funds? Well, that answer depends on the state. States are taking different approaches on the regulation of cryptocurrency, with some clarifying that the use of cryptocurrency to transfer funds from one person to another is within the statute, while others are taking the opposite position.[59] States that allow cryptocurrency firms to register under their money transmitting statutes are seeing applications filed by entities that wish to transmit money in digital currency form. For instance, popular U.S. based cryptocurrency exchange, Coinbase, currently holds licenses in 41 U.S. states and territories.[60] Cryptocurrency firms do not require a license to operate in states that have clarified their money transmitter statutes do not apply to cryptocurrencies.

There is a time and cost component to complying with the varied and occasionally conflicting state laws. Any entity attempting to operate on a nationwide basis may find that obtaining necessary state licenses can take one to two years or more. In addition, licensing and compliance may cost millions of dollars in legal, consulting, and other fees, not to mention the opportunity cost of having management's focus diverted away from building the business. Recognizing that cryptocurrency firms do not fit neatly into their existing money transmission statutes, the New York Department of Financial Services, or NY DFS, established a first-of-its-kind BitLicense which came into effect in 2015.[61] The BitLicense requires that those involved in "Virtual Currency Business Activity" in or involving the state of New York must apply for a unique license and adhere to the substantive requirements of the BitLicense. The BitLicense can be described as "money transmitter plus" because, in addition to imposing requirements similar to those imposed by money transmitter regulation, the BitLicense also imposes requirements tailored to the unique nature of the virtual currency business, such as cybersecurity and special suspicious activity reports.

To meet the requirements of the NY DFS, entities hoping to obtain a BitLicense must ensure they have a designated compliance officer to deal with issues such as anti-money laundering, have policies in place for customer complaints, and must also issue transactional receipts for potential audit. The application process is stringent and will cost approximately $5,000 to file. This will include compliance manuals; full transparency on ownership, finances and insurance; and a long-term business plan. Upon receiving the BitLicense, entities will be subject to ongoing supervision and must submit periodic financial statements.

The BitLicense excludes merchants and consumers that transact in digital currency, the development of software, digital currency "miners," and nonfinancial uses of digital currencies. Reactions to the New York BitLicense were mixed, with some observers arguing that it was an appropriate step to regulate a nascent industry that did not fit neatly into existing rules and regulations. However, the reaction within the cryptocurrency community was near unanimous, with most arguing that the BitLicense imposes an unnecessary regulatory burden that serves as a barrier to entry for new firms who most likely cannot afford the legal fees required to obtain the license.

In 2017, the National Conference of Commissioners on Uniform State Laws, also known as the Uniform Law Commission, released the Uniform Regulation of Virtual Currency Businesses Act, which was largely modeled off of the New York state BitLicense.[62] The Act is designed to provide for uniform state laws governing the operation of a business, wherever located, that engages in the virtual currency business. The Act contains a reciprocity provision that allows an entity licensed under one state statute to also do business in another state without applying for a virtual currency-specific license in that state if both states' statutes are based on the model Act. However, states are not required to enact the Uniform Law Commission's recommendations and to date, no state has adopted the Virtual Currency Businesses Act. As the virtual currency industry continues to evolve and mature, expect some states to adopt the Act or some version of it.

Regulating Cryptocurrency as a Commodity

The Commodity Futures Trading Commission (CFTC) is the agency responsible for overseeing U.S. commodities markets. Specifically, the CFTC aims to protect market users and their funds, consumers, and the public from fraud, manipulation, and abusive practices related to derivatives and other products that are subject to the Commodity Exchange Act. In 2015, the CFTC classified Bitcoin, and by extension other virtual currencies, as a commodity in an order against Coinflip Incorporated.[63] This order stated that Bitcoin and other virtual currencies fall under the definition of a commodity according to the Commodity Exchange Act of 1936. As a result of this order, virtual currencies are now considered "exempt commodities," which is the same category that the CFTC places metals and energies commodities, including: gold, silver, oil, and natural gas. The CFTC has jurisdiction over futures and other derivatives involving these exempt commodities but the cash markets, also referred to as the spot markets, for these commodities do not fall under the jurisdiction of the CFTC. However, the CFTC does have fraud and manipulation enforcement jurisdiction over these markets and market participants.[64]

Because the CFTC considers cryptocurrency to be a commodity and they do not regulate commodity spot markets, online exchanges like Coinbase do not need to register with the CFTC. However, any business involved in virtual currency derivatives— including foreign businesses that solicit or provide services to U.S. customers—will most likely have to register with the CFTC. In addition, if any entity offers a commodity, such as Bitcoin, for sale to a retail customer on a margined, leveraged, or financed basis – in other words, with borrowed funds – then the agreement is regulated as if it were a futures transaction unless the commodity is actually delivered to the buyer within 28 days.[65]

In December 2017, the Chicago Board Options Exchange and the Chicago Mercantile Exchange began listing Bitcoin futures contracts. Both these exchanges were able to list unique Bitcoin futures contracts after going through the CFTC's self-certification process, whereby the exchange verifies that a new contract complies with Commodity Exchange Act and CFTC regulations. Provided the CFTC does not object to the findings of the self-certification, the exchange is able to list a new product one day after submitting the self-certification. The introduction of Bitcoin futures was controversial, with many arguing that the CFTC should have intervened to halt the self-certification on the grounds that futures prices can be manipulated because Bitcoin is lightly traded compared to traditional asset classes.[66] The CFTC argues there was little they could do because the exchanges met all applicable requirements for self-certification.[67] In addition, the CFTC believes Bitcoin futures contracts will give them greater visibility into Bitcoin spot markets, which they do have the authority to police for fraud and manipulation. Regardless, the introduction of Bitcoin futures contracts was a pivotal moment in the history of cryptocurrency. For the first time, investors had access to a regulated and liquid instrument that allowed them to bet on the future price of Bitcoin without having to go through the process of purchasing actual Bitcoin.

Because the CFTC classifies virtual currency as a commodity, this means that it cannot also be a security subject to Securities and Exchange Commission (SEC) rules and regulations. However, any sort of investment vehicle that holds virtual currency and offers ownership interests in the vehicle will be considered a security subject to SEC registration unless it meets SEC exemption requirements. This is why the SEC must sign off before any sort of Bitcoin, or other virtual currency, Exchange Traded Fund can enter the market. Exchange Traded Funds, commonly referred to as ETFs, are simply marketable securities that track an index, a commodity, bonds, or a basket of assets like an index fund. Unlike mutual funds, an ETF trades like a common stock on a stock exchange. In 2017, the SEC rejected a bid by Bitcoin investors Cameron and Tyler Winklevoss to list an ETF tied to the price of Bitcoin.[68] The SEC's main concern was the unregulated nature of Bitcoin spot markets made the ETF susceptible to fraud and manipulation.

After Bitcoin futures came to market, the SEC received a flood of new ETF applications that all proposed to track the price of Bitcoin futures. Once again, the SEC rejected these proposals due to concerns over the potential for fraud and manipulation in the Bitcoin spot market. However, the SEC went a step further and listed a series of questions that must be satisfactorily answered by the ETF sponsor before the agency will authorize a virtual currency related ETF.[69] First, will investment funds have the information necessary to adequately value crypto currencies or crypto currency related products given their volatility, the fragmentation and general lack of regulation of underlying cryptocurrency markets, and the nascent state and current trading volume in the cryptocurrency futures markets? Second, what steps would funds investing in cryptocurrencies or cryptocurrency related products take to assure that they would have sufficiently liquid assets to meet redemptions daily? Third, to the extent the fund plans to hold crypto currency directly, how would it satisfy requirements to properly safeguard these assets? The SEC made clear that until these questions can be satisfactorily answered, it would be inappropriate for fund sponsors to initiate registration of funds that intend to invest substantially in cryptocurrency and related products.

Because much of the SEC's concerns revolve around the fact that cryptocurrency spot markets are unregulated, some within the cryptocurrency community have called on the industry to police itself.[70] To this end, Tyler and Cameron Winklevoss who run the Gemini exchange for trading Bitcoin and Ether, have submitted a proposal to create the Virtual Commodity Association, a self-regulatory organization meant to police digital-currency markets and custodians.[71] The Virtual Commodity Association would be a nonprofit group with the aim to develop industry standards, promote transparency, and work with regulators, including the CFTC to prevent fraud. While self-regulatory organizations exist in other industries, most notably the Financial Industry Regulatory Authority for the securities industry, the Winklevoss proposal is unlikely to gain much traction due to the fragmented nature of the cryptocurrency industry and the industry's historical aversion to any kind of central authority.

Regulating Cryptocurrency as Property

In 2014, the IRS announced that it would treat virtual currencies as property rather than currency under federal tax law.[72] Tax authorities in some states have followed suit and announced that virtual currencies will be treated as property under their state tax laws. Thus, purchases and sales of virtual currency, and payments made with virtual currency, can be taxable events. Accordingly, if you were to buy a cup coffee with Bitcoin, that would technically be a taxable event, and you would have to pay taxes on the amount that Bitcoin increased by from the time you purchased it to the time you bought your coffee. There is currently a bill circulating in Congress that would change this tax treatment by exempting small gains from certain sales or exchanges of virtual currency from a taxpayer's gross income.[73] While the bill's prospects are uncertain, its passage would make it more viable to use virtual currency as a method of payment for most transactions.

Currently, if an investor sells a virtual currency after holding it longer than a year, then the profits under the IRS's classification are typically treated as long-term capital gains, and the tax rate will therefore be 0%, 15%, or 20%, plus a 3.8% surtax in some cases, depending on the owner's total income. Short-term gains on cryptocurrencies, held a year or less, are typically taxable at higher ordinary income rates.

While cryptocurrency does provide a greater degree of anonymity compared to traditional fiat currency, this does not mean that your cryptocurrency transactions will go unnoticed by the IRS. In 2016, the IRS demanded that the largest U.S. based cryptocurrency exchange, Coinbase, turn over all records pertaining to any U.S. person who conducted transactions in a convertible virtual currency between January 1, 2013, and December 31, 2015.[74] After a yearlong lawsuit, the IRS won a judgment that forced Coinbase to turn over account records for more than 14,000 customers.[75] More recently, in January 2018, Coinbase sent 1099-K forms to a number of its current users informing them that their trading proceeds were being reported to the IRS and reminding them to pay the taxes they owed.[76]

Explaining Initial Coin Offerings

Initial coin offerings (ICOs) allow companies to raise money by creating and selling a digital token on a blockchain in exchange for cryptocurrency – typically Bitcoin or Ether. Some blockchain tokens function as a digital currency. Other tokens can represent a right to tangible assets like gold or real estate. Blockchain tokens can also be used in new protocols and networks to create distributed applications, and these tokens are sometimes referred to as app coins, utility tokens or protocol tokens. And then there are some initial coin offerings that are intended to be nothing more than a speculative venture. Most initial coin offerings are conducted on the Ethereum blockchain, which was designed to support decentralized applications.

From an issuer standpoint, the biggest benefit in conducting an ICO is that it provides an economic incentive for a network to get off the ground and overcome the classic chicken-and-egg problem. In other words, it gives all users of an app or software the ability to own a little piece of the network, incentivizing them to start using it from the beginning. This gives the network a higher chance of success with a lot less initial capital needed.

There are essentially two types of ICOs: pre-release and post-release. Pre-release ICOs have historically been the more common, and can be conducted in fiat, digital currency, or some combination of the two. As the name implies, pre-release ICOs occur when a project needs funds to develop a product or service. Post-release ICOs occur when a project has launched an initial version of their protocol and corresponding token and wants additional funds to continue its development.

If a company wants to issue an ICO, they should follow the following steps.[4] Step 1 is to publish a detailed whitepaper that describes the network you are trying to build and what it will be used for. The whitepaper should provide a clear and compelling reason for the digital token to exist, provide a detailed technical description of the proposed project implementation, and set clear expectations for total token supply and distribution. Step 2 is to provide a detailed development roadmap that will include estimates of time and cost for each stage of the project, and the names of key members of the development team and their advisors. The roadmap should allocate funding for each stage of development and consider restricting access to funding until milestones are achieved. Step 3 is to use an open, public, blockchain and publish all the code for your project. This provides transparency and enables real participation from token holders and independent developers. Step 4 is to use clear, logical and fair pricing in the token sale. This includes

---

[4] Note that I said should; not all ICOs will follow these exact steps, but doing so will help maximize the funds raised while also staying on the right side of the applicable regulations.

setting the maximum number of tokens to be sold in a crowd sale and using a pricing mechanism which does not increase over time. Step 5 is to determine the percentage of tokens to be set aside for the development team to reward them for the work they put into the project. And the final step, or warning if you will, is to refrain from marketing the token as an investment. Tokens promoted as investments most likely qualify as securities subject to SEC registration.

Prior to 2017, Initial Coin Offerings were essentially unheard of. Figure 4.2 shows that at the beginning of 2017, there had been $300 million raised all-time through ICOs. By the end of 2017, $5.86 billion had been raised through ICOs. In December of 2017 alone, $1.4 billion was raised through ICOs.

Figure 4.2

All-Time Cumulative ICO Funding

Data Source: Coindesk All-Time Cumulative ICO Funding

This remarkable growth in ICOs is hard to explain. Certainly the massive increase in the value of cryptocurrencies that occurred in 2017 played a big role, as did greater familiarity with, and adoption of, blockchain technology. However, just like with cryptocurrencies, human psychology has played a major role. Many people have been buying ICOs simply because they think they can sell it for a higher price later and could care less about the tokens underlying utility. However, this is an extremely risky strategy as a Boston College study found that approximately 56% of startups that raise money through ICOs die within four months of their token offering.[77] If the SEC were to deem all ICOs to be securities subject to SEC registration, the ICO market would crumble. However, the SEC has taken a more measured approach to regulating ICOs thus far.

Regulatory Framework for Initial Coin Offerings

The key question for any ICO is: does it meet the SEC's definition of a security? If the answer is yes, then a whole slew of regulatory requirements kick-in and the purpose of the ICO, which is to raise start-up funds at minimal cost, is defeated. But the SEC has yet to provide a bright line test that would allow market participants to know for certain if their proposed ICO would qualify as a security. However, the agency has left hints through various enforcement actions and public statements that market participants are relying on to structure ICOs in such a way that they think is exempt from security classification. But these market participants may be wrong and could one day find themselves on the other side of an SEC enforcement action that accuses them of violating U.S. securities laws. Thus, it is critical for any entity who is considering issuing an ICO to be aware of applicable securities laws and to think seriously about the potential consequences of violating these laws.

When you think of a financial security, you probably think of things like stocks and bonds, which are clearly different from ICOs. But section 2 of the Securities Act of 1933 provides a broad definition, which includes something known as an investment contract.[78] Thus, the key question for determining whether or not an ICO is a security is: does the ICO qualify as an investment contract? The Securities Act did not establish clear guidelines for what constitutes an investment contract, which is why it ultimately fell to the Supreme Court, in the 1946 case of SEC vs. Howey, to establish a test for determining whether or not certain transactions qualify as investment contracts.[79] In what's become known as the Howey Test, the Court stated a transaction is an investment contract if: it is an investment of money, there is an expectation of profits from the investment, the investment of money is in a common enterprise, and any profit comes from the efforts of a promoter or third-party. If all four of these factors are met, the transaction is an investment contract and therefore a security that needs to be registered with the SEC or qualify for an exemption from SEC registration requirements.

Registering with the SEC takes time and is costly, and is obviously something most ICO issuers want to avoid. The problem is that issuers can't know for certain if their ICO satisfies all four prongs of the Howey test in the eyes of the SEC. In July of 2017, the SEC provided some guidance on how they view ICOs when they released a report of investigation that looked at one specific ICO known as the Decentralized Autonomous Organization (DAO.)[80] The DAO was created by a group of people working for a company called Slock.it who wrote the smart contract that ran the DAO. Smart contracts are computer protocols that are intended to facilitate, verify, and enforce negotiation of a contract without the need for third-parties. Between April 30th and May 28th of 2016, the DAO offered and sold approximately 1.15 billion digital tokens in exchange for a total of approximately 12 million Ether, which had a value of $150 million at the time. All of this was done on the Ethereum blockchain. After the funding period, the DAO began to operate, whereby various people made proposals to the DAO on how to spend the funds raised and the members who bought the tokens voted to approve these proposals. If these proposals were profitable, DAO token holders were entitled a proportional share of the reward.

The SEC assessed the facts and circumstances around the DAO and determined that it was an investment contract according to the Howey Test. First, the SEC determined that the DAO was an investment of money because it accepted the cryptocurrency Ether. The SEC has long held that cash is not the only form of contribution or investment that will create an investment contract and in their DAO report, the SEC expanded the definition of money to include cryptocurrencies. Second, the SEC found that various promotional materials disseminated by Slock.It and its co-founders clearly stated the DAO was a for-profit entity whose objective was to fund projects in exchange for a return on investment. Therefore, there was a clear expectation of profits by DAO investors. Third, the SEC deemed the DAO to be a common enterprise because multiple investors pooled funds into the DAO and the profits of each investor were correlated with those of the other investors. And finally, the SEC found that any profit from the DAO was determined by the efforts of Slock.It and its co-founders, and not the investors. Projects to be voted on by all DAO token holders were selected by a group of curators affiliated with Slock.it. In addition, each individual token holder was anonymous and really didn't have much control over what the DAO did. Therefore, the DAO's investors relied on the managerial and entrepreneurial efforts of Slock.it and its co-founders, and The DAO's Curators, to manage The DAO and put forth project proposals that could generate profits for The DAO's investors.

Although the SEC found that the DAO met all four factors of the Howey Test and was therefore a security, the DAO never registered with the SEC because shortly after launching, the DAO was hacked and all the Ether it had raised was stolen.[81] Nonetheless, the SEC's report of investigation on the DAO, while not an official regulation, serves as a guidepost for all other ICO issuers to help them determine whether or not they need to register their ICO with the SEC.

It may be possible that all ICOs qualify as securities. In fact, in February 2018, SEC chairman Jay Clayton stated that every ICO he'd seen was a security.[82] But until more formal SEC guidance is issued, ICO issuers must rely on the DAO report of investigation and SEC enforcement actions against other ICO issuers to help guide them. Based upon what we know now, for an ICO not to be considered a security, it would require at a minimum: a truly decentralized structure, without curators, gatekeepers, and reliance on management; no profit intention; restrictions or significant controls on secondary trading; token purchasers are given meaningful control over the voting, operation, promotion and safekeeping of the enterprise; and token purchasers are provided all information necessary to make an informed decision.

Some prominent observers have begun to apply the Howey test to several cryptocurrencies, specifically Ether and XRP, and have argued that they also qualify as securities.[83] This argument primarily hinges on whether or not these currencies are part of a common enterprise. Given that Ether was introduced by the Ethereum Foundation and XRP by Ripple Labs and that both these entities continue to play a critical role in promoting their currency, a credible argument can be made that they meet the Howey test and are therefore securities. However, in June of 2018, the SEC stated publicly that Ether was not a security (they have yet to officially comment on XRP.)[84] For now, the majority of cryptocurrencies qualify as commodities and not securities.

Because of the uncertainty that surrounds the security status of ICOs, a document has been developed by legal professionals in the cryptocurrency industry known as the Simple Agreement for Future Token, or SAFT.[85] If a developer believes that any tokens sold in the future will be a utility token, meaning they entitle the holder to specific services or units of services, a SAFT contract can be created as a security and sold to accredited investors. This contract ensures investors that tokens will be delivered to them once a functioning network or application has been developed and tokens can be used on it. The bet that issuers and investors of a SAFT are making is that the SEC or the courts will determine that the tokens are not securities at this later point in time, while they might have been classified as such during the ICO, because there was no fully functional network or no use value yet. Even though tokens issued using a SAFT are more likely to escape SEC security classification, the SEC has not officially confirmed that this two-step framework will work as intended.

Outside of the report of investigation on the DAO, most of the SEC's involvement with ICOs has been through the enforcement process. In September of 2017, the SEC's Enforcement Division created a new cyber unit to focus the Enforcement Division's substantial cyber-related expertise on targeting cyber-related misconduct, including violations involving distributed ledger technology and initial coin offerings.[86] In 2017, the SEC took five enforcement actions against cryptocurrency and initial coin offering firms. As of July 1st, 2018, they've taken six enforcement actions with more sure to come.[87]

The SEC has also warned cryptocurrency exchanges that they risk operating illegally if they are selling securities and are not registered as a securities exchange with the SEC.[88] Many of the websites where you can buy and sell cryptocurrency refer to themselves as exchanges, which can give the misimpression to investors that they are regulated or meet the regulatory standards of a national securities exchange. Platforms that decide to register with the SEC have at least two options: accept strict regulations that apply to public markets, like the New York Stock Exchange, or lighter touch rules that cover alternative trading systems, which are private trading venues, run by brokers such as Morgan Stanley. Registered exchanges have to enforce rules against fraud and manipulation and are prohibited from cutting deals that give certain customers advantages over others. Some of the best-known platforms for trading digital assets, including Coinbase's G-Dax platform, limit their order books to only well-known cryptocurrencies like Bitcoin and Ether, which have been deemed commodities by the government. These platforms are effectively free from SEC oversight because they don't offer investments the SEC regulates. However, in June of 2018, Coinbase announced that through a series of acquisitions, they had acquired a broker dealer license, an alternative trading system license, and a registered investment advisor license.[89] If approved by the SEC, Coinbase will be allowed to offer Blockchain-based securities, like SEC registered initial coin offerings.

The SEC has also warned that platforms offering digital wallet services, which are used to safe keep digital assets, could run afoul of laws that apply to brokerage firms and other regulated entities that keep track of owners securities.

Chapter 5: FinTech Payments, Wealth Management, and Account Aggregation

Traditional Payment Systems

Imagine the year is 1998 and Kate walks into her local Starbucks to buy a cup of coffee. To pay for her coffee, Kate has four options: cash, credit card, debit card, or personal check. Now fast forward twenty years to 2018 and Kate still loves her Starbucks. Now when she walks into the store, she has a multitude of payment options available to her. She can still pay with cash, credit card or debit card; or she can pay with the Starbucks Mobile App, Chase Pay, Apple Pay, PayPal, or Visa Checkout.[90] However, one option available to Kate in 1998, personal check, is no longer accepted by Starbucks – which is probably appreciated by the people waiting in line behind her.

All these payment options have different implications for Kate and for Starbucks. For Kate, her choice of payment determines whether she can rescind the transaction, whether her money is at risk if her account is compromised, and whether she is exposed to overdraft or limit fees. For Starbucks, Kate's choice of payment determines when they will receive value for her purchase and the amount of, if any, transaction fees they must pay.

Behind each of these payment methods is a unique system with its own procedures and rules that transfers value from the customer's financial intermediary to the merchant's financial intermediary. Many new payment technologies run atop the rails of older payments infrastructure and therefore fit within established legal frameworks that govern various payment methods, while other new technologies, such as payments sent through distributed ledger technology, utilize entirely new networks that are not subject to a well-defined legal framework.

As you might imagine, how Americans pay for goods and services has evolved dramatically over the past twenty years. Figure 5.1 utilizes data from the Federal Reserve's Diary of Consumer Payment Choice (DCPC), which tracks consumer payment transactions over a three-day period for a representative sample of consumers. Cash remains the most frequently used payment instrument, accounting for 31% of all consumer transactions, while debit card is the second most frequently used payment method, accounting for 27% of payments volume. However, cash payments accounted for just 8% of the value of consumer purchases while electronic payments, in the form of electronic credit and debit transfers using the automated clearinghouse system, account for 32% of the value of all transactions.

Figure 5.1

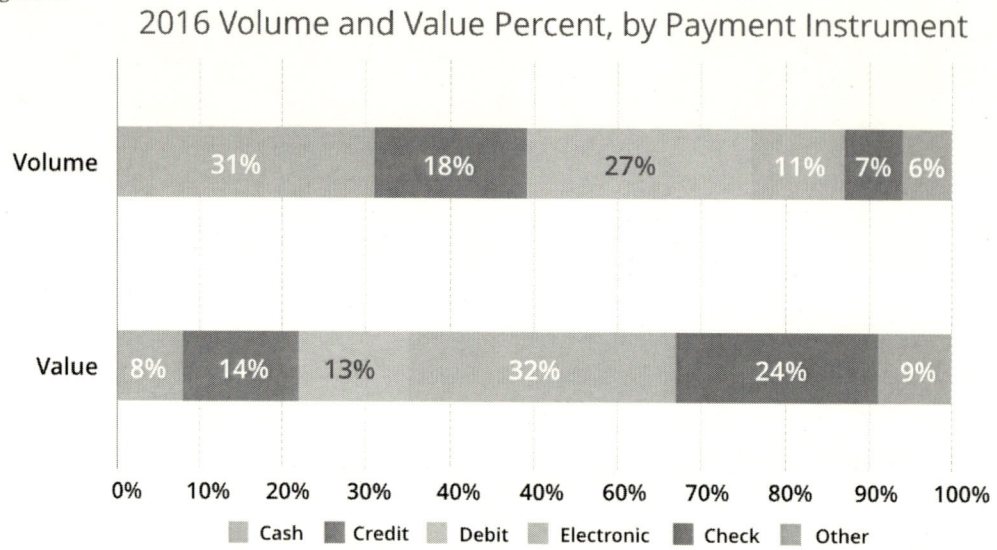

2016 Volume and Value Percent, by Payment Instrument

	Cash	Credit	Debit	Electronic	Check	Other
Volume	31%	18%	27%	11%	7%	6%
Value	8%	14%	13%	32%	24%	9%

Federal Reserve's Diary of Consumer Payment Choice (DCPC)

These results imply that the value of the payment appears to influence whether a consumer chooses to use cash, debit, credit, or another form of payment. Figure 5.2 shows that cash is used most often for payments less than $25, while credit and debit cards are used more frequently for payments valued between $25 and $100. Checks and electronic payments are used more frequently for transactions valued at $100 and over.[5]

---

[5] Fintech payment platforms, such as Venmo, are part of the "Other" category, which accounts for a small share of payments volume and value as shown in Figure 5.2

Figure 5.2

Payment Use by Amount 2016

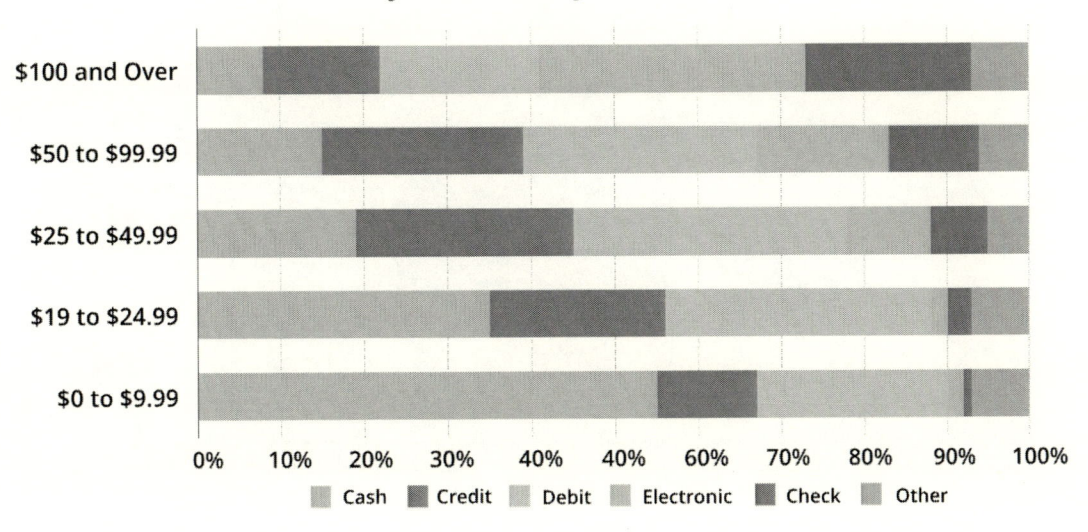

[Bar chart showing payment method breakdown by transaction amount ranges: $100 and Over, $50 to $99.99, $25 to $49.99, $19 to $24.99, $0 to $9.99. Categories: Cash, Credit, Debit, Electronic, Check, Other.]

Federal Reserve's Diary of Consumer Payment Choice (DCPC)

The Starbucks example demonstrates that consumer payment preferences have evolved over time. Figure 5.3 utilizes data from a separate Federal Reserve Study that reports the aggregate number of various noncash payments that have been made by U.S. consumers and businesses over time. In 2003, checks were the most common noncash payment method, accounting for close to half of all noncash transactions. The digital revolution quickly made checks obsolete, and today checks account for just under 13% of all noncash transactions. As sharply as checks have fallen, debit cards have risen. Today, debit cards account for 59% of all noncash transactions while credit cards are the next most popular payment method, accounting for 24% of all noncash payment transactions by businesses and consumers.

Figure 5.3

Non-cash Payment Transactions by Payment Type

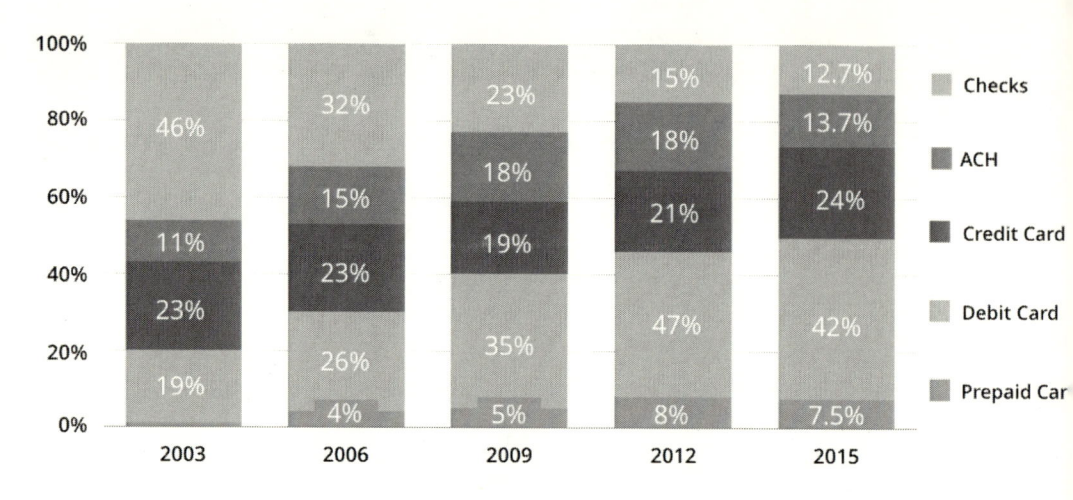

	2003	2006	2009	2012	2015
Checks	46%	32%	23%	15%	12.7%
ACH	11%	15%	18%	18%	13.7%
Credit Card	23%	23%	19%	21%	24%
Debit Card	19%	26%	35%	47%	42%
Prepaid Card		4%	5%	8%	7.5%

The Federal Reserve Payments Study

Different laws, rules and regulations govern all of these payment methods. The laws governing payment systems are passed by the U.S. Congress and state legislatures, and regulations are then established by federal and state agencies to implement these laws. In addition, payment system operators and providers have established their own rules and agreements that provide more details on the rights and obligations of the users of the payment system. These frameworks are designed with one purpose in mind, to facilitate settlement. Settlement simply means that whatever is purchased is delivered to the buyer and the payment for said purchase is made to the seller. While this may sound straightforward, achieving settlement is a complicated process.

The initiation of a payment begins when either the payer or payee in a payment transaction, or a third-party, sends an instruction to another entity that triggers a process ultimately leading to a payment. The first step in this process is to authenticate the identity or veracity of a participant, device, payment, or message connected to a payment system. Authentication may happen at multiple points in the payment process. For example, end-user identity may be verified when the end user enrolls with a provider or additional checks may be built in to verify the identity of the payer, account, or account provider (for instance by entering a password) during the payment process. During the authentication process, the payer's account provider verifies that the payer's account has good funds or credit necessary to complete the transaction. From there the payment is authorized, which involves explicit instructions, including timing, amount, payee, source of funds and other conditions given by the payer to their account provider or to the payee to transfer funds on a one-time or recurring basis. The next step is to clear the payment, which involves the payer's and payee's account providers exchanging payment information to confirm a transaction prior to settlement. Then comes receipt, which is the point when funds are received by the payee, such that the funds can be withdrawn or transferred. Next comes settlement – which in some payment systems comes before receipt – where obligations in respect of funds between two or more entities are discharged. And finally, the payment is reconciled, meaning a procedure is followed to verify that the records issued by entities involved in a transaction match.

Note that each payment method uses a slightly different processing approach and may not follow all of the steps above or in the order mentioned. Nonetheless, these steps reflect the general process a payment goes through to achieve settlement. With that in mind, it is worth examining two of the oldest payment methods in the U.S. – cash and check.

While the government is required to accept cash as valid payment, there is no law that requires private individuals or businesses to accept cash or coins as payment. Therefore, cash is a trust-based system that works so long as the public has confidence in it. Cash is a preferred form of payment for many people because it does not require or record the identity of end users. Until the launch of Bitcoin, cash was the only payment instrument with such features. The main risk associated with using cash is theft or loss, and this risk is born entirely by the holder of cash. However, this loss is limited to the amount of cash the owner actually carries. When you use cash to pay for goods, say a carton of milk at the store, settlement is achieved the moment you hand your cash to the cashier and he hands you the milk.

Checks on the other hand, achieve settlement by moving funds from the payer's bank to the payee's bank by decreasing the payer's account balance and increasing that of the payee's. Imagine again the year is 1998 and Kate pays for her Starbucks with personal check. Settlement is achieved through the following steps. First, Starbucks deposits Kate's check and Starbucks' bank credits Starbucks' account. Starbucks' bank in turn presents the check to its regional Federal Reserve Bank, which credits Starbuck's bank's account at the Federal Reserve and passes the obligation on to Kate's bank. The Federal Reserve Bank then debits the account that Kate's bank maintains at the Federal Reserve Bank. Finally, Kate's bank satisfies the claim by debiting the amount from Kate's account.

While checks are becoming a less frequent form of payment, the process by which checks are settled is similar for all noncash payment systems. In essence, settlement is achieved by updating ledgers at different financial intermediaries to adjust deposit balances in accordance with the transfer of claims as they move along the chain from payer to payee accounts.

Checking is governed by both state and federal law. At the state level, checks are negotiable instruments subject to provisions of the Uniform Commercial Code, which was established to make it easier for businesses in different states to do business with each other. At the Federal Level, checking is governed by provisions of the Expedited Funds Availability Act and the Check Clearing for the 21st Century Act, (also known as "Check 21").

The Expedited Funds Availability Act requires banks to make funds available to accountholders within specified timeframes and to disclose their policies on funds availability.[91] Federal Reserve Regulation CC is the regulation that implements the Act.[92] Check 21 allows the recipient of the original paper check to create a digital version of the original check, thereby eliminating the need for further handling of the physical document.[93] In essence, the recipient bank no longer returns the paper check, but effectively e-mails an image of both sides of the check to the bank it is drawn upon. Another effect of the law is that it is now legal for anyone to use a computer scanner or mobile phone to capture images of checks and deposit them electronically, a process known as remote deposit.

Unlike cash, checks do not settle instantaneously, which therefore exposes depository institutions to the risks of nonpayment and fraud. Generally speaking, the laws and regulations governing checking require banks to bear the responsibility for losses that would be difficult for another party to avoid, such as a loss arising from an unauthorized check. Debit cards are subject to many of the same laws and regulations that apply to checking.

Card Based Payments and Interbank Transfers

Credit cards and debit cards have the same basic electronic payment structure, meaning they operate through a card network, with the most common networks being Visa and MasterCard. Visa and MasterCard serve as intermediaries in an open-loop process, meaning the card can be used to pay for goods anywhere the processing brand is accepted. Visa and MasterCard do not issue any credit cards. Rather, they license their payment brands to issuers and acquirers. Issuing banks are the entities that provide consumers with the credit cards in their pocket. Acquirers are the entities— or merchants — that process the transactions. American Express and Discover are a bit different in that they serve as both intermediaries and card-issuing creditors.

When Kate swipes her Visa credit card at the Starbucks terminal, information is transmitted to the bank that issued the card to Kate so that the bank can determine the validity of the card and the availability of credit sufficient to complete the transaction –all this happens near instantaneously. At the end of each business day, Starbucks will send all approved authorizations in a batch to their bank who in turn routes this information to the Visa network for settlement. The credit card network forwards each approved transaction to the appropriate issuing bank and then usually within 24 to 48 hours of the transaction, the issuing bank will transfer the funds less an "interchange fee," which it shares with the credit card network. The credit card network then pays Starbucks' bank who in turn credits Starbucks' account. Finally, the issuing bank posts the transaction to Kate's account and sends her the monthly bill.

Card network rules and federal law govern credit card transactions. For a bank to issue or a merchant to accept a card brand – be it Visa, American Express, or some other brand – it must affiliate with the card network and agree to the rules by which it operates. Some of these rules directly benefit consumers, and others can be relied on by banks to provide consumers with protections that exceed those required by law. The most widely advertised protection mandated by the card networks is a "zero liability" policy for fraudulent transactions. Both Visa and MasterCard require that all of their branded products (including credit, debit, and prepaid cards) carry this protection.

Credit card transactions are also governed by federal law, specifically the Credit Card Responsibility and Disclosure Act, or CARD Act, and the Truth in Lending Act. The CARD Act was enacted in 2009 to "establish fair and transparent practices related to the extension of credit" in the credit card market, thereby regulating both the underwriting and pricing of credit card accounts.[94] The CARD Act prohibits credit card issuers from extending credit without assessing the consumer's ability to pay and restricts the amount of "upfront" fees that an issuer can charge during the first year after an account is opened. It also limits the instances in which issuers can charge "back-end" penalty fees when a consumer makes a late payment or exceeds his or her credit limit. The CARD Act also restricts the circumstances under which issuers can increase interest rates on credit cards and establishes procedures for doing so.

The Truth in Lending Act, or TILA, was passed in 1968 after Congress determined that consumers needed assistance in understanding important credit terms and protections against various creditor practices deemed to be unfair.[95] Implemented by Regulation Z, which is jointly enforced by the Federal Reserve and the Consumer Financial Protection Bureau, TILA protects consumers from liability for charges resulting from the unauthorized use of their credit cards, requires creditors to investigate and promptly correct billing errors that consumers allege have occurred in connection with their accounts, and entitles consumers to maintain against a creditor similar claims that they might assert against a merchant in connection with the purchase of defective or otherwise unsatisfactory goods and services.[96]

Unlike credit cards, debit cards don't involve interest rate worries, monthly bills, or finance charges; since they only use the money you actually have in your bank account. A disadvantage of debit cards is the amount of buying protection provided to you by law. Debit card transactions very much resemble cash transactions. The money changes hands quickly, and it's difficult to get it back. If you want to return a broken or unsatisfactory item you purchased with a debit card, many businesses will only give you an exchange or store credit. The laws that govern stolen debit cards aren't as friendly as the laws that govern stolen credit cards, as a result you may find it more difficult to get your money back if an unauthorized transaction occurs.

Debit card transactions are regulated by the Electronic Fund Transfer Act– or EFTA – and it's implementing regulation, Regulation E. The EFTA defines an electronic fund transfer as "any transfer of funds, other than a transaction originated by check,… which is initiated through an electronic terminal, telephonic instrument, or computer so as to order, instruct, or authorize a financial institution to debit or credit an account. The term includes, but is not limited to, point-of-sale transfers, ATM transactions, direct deposits or withdrawals of funds, and transfers initiated by telephone."[97]

Regulation E establishes rights and responsibilities for consumers as it pertains to Electronic fund transfers. For lost or stolen debit cards, Regulation E stipulates that as long as you report your card stolen within two days, you won't lose more than $50 of the money a thief draws on our account. If you report it after two days but within sixty days, you could be liable for as much as $500. And if you report it outside of 60 days, you face unlimited liability. However, Visa and MasterCard, as well as many card issuing banks, may not hold you liable for debit transactions you did not authorize.

Credit and debit card transactions achieve settlement by routing through the banking system, which requires the payer to have a bank account. But what about consumers who don't have access to a bank account? In 2015, approximately 15.6 million adults in the U.S. did not have a checking or savings account.[98] An additional 51.1 million adults were underbanked, meaning that they had an account at an insured institution but also obtained financial services and products outside the banking system.[99] For these people, conducting payments can be challenging, with many of them using cash more frequently than your average consumer and incurring high fees to use other noncash payment systems, such as money transfers.

One payment option available to these consumers are prepaid cards, which are like a debit card except they are not linked to an individually owned bank account. Prepaid cards have grown in popularity in recent years and now account for 7.5% of all noncash transactions. Some employers are paying their employees who don't have bank accounts by issuing them general purpose prepaid cards that run on the Visa or MasterCard network. In addition, many state and federal government assistance programs issue benefits through prepaid cards. For many years, the regulatory framework applicable to prepaid cards was different from that of debit cards, with consumers having far fewer protections available to them. But in 2016, the Consumer Financial Protection Bureau finalized a rule that gives prepaid account consumers important protections under the Electronic Fund Transfer Act; protections that are similar to those for checking accounts and debit cards.[100] They include: free and easy access to account information, error resolution rights, and protections for lost cards and unauthorized transactions.

The unbanked and underbanked have historically been frequent users of money transfer services, such as those provided by companies like Western Union. Many foreigners and new immigrants use money transmitters to send money home to support their families and relatives. These cross-border payments, known as remittances, totaled $575 billion in 2016.[101] Remittances take much longer to process than domestic payments and carry much higher transaction fees. A payment often goes through a complex network of international and intermediary banks (each charging a fee) before it reaches the final recipient. The World Bank estimates that the global average cost of sending a $200 remittance at the end of 2017 was $14.26.[102] New FinTech payment developments carry the potential to lower these costs.

In the U.S., states have their own money transmitter laws and examine transmitters through their state banking departments. In fact, until passage of the Dodd-Frank Act in 2010, no federal consumer protection law directly regulated foreign remittance transfers. This changed when Congress amended the Electronic Fund Transfer Act in the Dodd-Frank Act to add a new section to the EFTA which created four new compliance requirements for foreign remittance transfers.[103] These include the establishment of: disclosures about important transaction terms, error resolution, and cancellation; error resolution procedures; cancellation and refund policies; and a remittance transfer provider's liability for the acts of its agents. The CFPB has amended regulation E several times to implement these new requirements.

Most of the payment methods mention thus far involve, at some point, the transfer of funds between the payer's bank and the payee's bank. It is important to understand how these interbank funds transfers occur because several FinTech payment applications are designed to integrate into this framework or supplant it entirely.

Interbank funds transfer systems are arrangements through which funds transfers are made between banks for their own account or on behalf of their customers. They are built on private contract or statute, with common rules and standardized procedures. There are two types of interbank funds transfer systems, retail, and wholesale. Retail funds transfer systems handle a large volume of payments of relatively low value in such forms as checks, credit transfers, automated clearing house transactions and electronic funds transfers at the point of sale. The average size of transfers through wholesale funds transfer systems is substantial and the transfers are typically more time critical, mostly because many of the payments are in settlement of financial market transactions.

In the U.S., the most prevalent retail interbank funds transfer system is The Automated Clearing House (ACH). ACH moves money and information from one bank account to another through Direct Deposit and Direct Payment via ACH transactions, including ACH credit and debit transactions; recurring and one-time payments; government, consumer, and business-to-business transactions; and international payments. Each year, ACH transfers over $43 trillion dollars through more than 25 billion electronic financial transactions.[104]

An ACH transfer begins when an originator – whether it's an individual, a corporation or another entity – initiates either a Direct Deposit or Direct Payment transaction using the ACH Network. These ACH entries are entered and transmitted electronically and can be either debit or credit payments and commonly include Direct Deposit of payroll, government and Social Security benefits, mortgage and bill payments, online banking payments, person-to-person, and business-to-business payments. Initiation occurs when the originator notifies their depository institution. The depository institution will then aggregate payments from customers and transmit them in batches at regular, predetermined intervals to an ACH Operator. One of two ACH operators, either the Federal Reserve or The Clearing House, will receive batches of ACH entries from the originating depository institution. The ACH transactions are then sorted and made available by the ACH operator to the receiving depository financial institution. Then the receiver's account is debited or credited by the receiving depository financial institution according to the type of ACH entry. Individuals, businesses, and other entities can all be receivers. Each ACH credit transaction settles in one to two business days, and each debit transaction settles in just one business day.

ACH payments are regulated by the Electronic Fund Transfer Act and its implementing regulation, Regulation E. In addition, the Electronic Payments Association, known as NACHA, is a self-governing, not-for-profit institution that establishes common rules and standards for ACH payments. These rules and standards govern the rights and obligations of banks that use the ACH network.

Some key points to keep in mind are that under Regulation E, if an unauthorized transfer occurs, then the consumer is not liable for that payment absent certain conditions. In addition, unlike credit card law, the NACHA Rules do not permit later rejection of a credit entry for reasons such as the originator's – or seller's – unsatisfactory performance of an underlying contractual obligation; which basically means that a buyer can't stop or reverse a transaction if he is not happy with the goods purchased or the performance of the seller.

Finally, it is worth mentioning that the two major wholesale interbank funds transfer systems in the U.S. are Fedwire and CHIPS. If you've ever had to send a bank wire, it's likely gone through one of these two systems. Fedwire is operated by the Federal Reserve and allows depository institutions and certain other financial institutions that hold an account with a Federal Reserve Bank to instruct the Federal Reserve to debit funds from its own account and credit funds to the account of another participant. Participants may originate funds transfers online, by initiating a secure electronic message, or off-line, via telephone procedures. Each transfer is final and irrevocable when a receiving depository institution is notified of it. Payment transactions over the Federal Reserve's Fedwire funds transfer system are governed by the Federal Reserve's Regulation J, which defines the rights and responsibilities of financial institutions that use Fedwire, as well as the rights and responsibilities of the Federal Reserve.[105]

The Clearing House Interbank Payments System, or CHIPS, is the primary clearing house in the U.S. for large banking transactions and is operated by the Clearing House Association. The payments transferred over CHIPS are often related to international interbank transactions, including the dollar payments resulting from foreign currency transactions. Under CHIPS, participating depository institutions exchange information throughout the day about individual transfers. The CHIPS system takes the orders and continuously tries to match or net these orders against offsetting orders. These payment orders are settled on the books of CHIPS, who in turn has a prefunded account to facilitate this settlement at the Federal Reserve Bank of New York.

Funds transfers made through CHIPS are subject to CHIPS rules and procedures.[106] CHIPS rules stipulate that the laws of the state of New York, which include Article 4A of the Uniform Commercial Code, apply to CHIPS transactions. In addition, Federal Reserve Regulation CC also regulates the time within which a depository institution receiving a Fedwire or CHIPS funds transfer on behalf of a customer must make those funds available to their customer.[107]

This information is complex, and you may be wondering why it is important. As confusing as it may be, the U.S.'s fragmented payments system is precisely why there is so much potential for FinTech payment firms. Many FinTech firms are attempting to build on top of the current framework, in order to improve the customer experience or provide needed efficiencies. Other FinTech firms, primarily those using distributed ledger technology, are attempting to bypass this system all together and start from scratch. Regardless of the future path of the U.S. payments industry, there is widespread recognition that things need to change.

Mobile Payment Developments

With the launch of so many alternative payment instruments since the financial crisis, consumers now enjoy unprecedented options when it comes to paying for goods and services. These include tools that allow customers to pay in-store with their mobile phones, make payments via social media, and send instant person-to-person transfers between bank accounts or debit cards. While these tools enhance customer convenience, they also produce new risks.

Many of these new payment tools work as an app on smartphones, and they are often linked to a user's existing debit or credit cards and are processed through the networks and channels for these types of payments. In some cases, FinTech providers may also route their payments through the Automated Clearing House networks, which have traditionally been used to facilitate automatic bill payments or funds transfers between banks. FinTech payments can also be made by charging a consumer's mobile phone bill. Perhaps you have donated money to the Red Cross or some other charity though text message, which ultimately showed up in your phone bill.

Table 5.1 highlights the growth in mobile payments over the past few years. In 2015, 24% of respondents in a Federal Reserve survey reported using mobile payments within the past 12 months, which is double the amount who reported using mobile payments in 2011. Unsurprisingly, use of mobile payments is most prevalent amongst younger consumers, with 32% of respondents ages 30 to 44 and 30% of respondents ages 18 to 29 reporting using mobile payments within the past 12 months.

Table 5.1

Use of Mobile Payments in the Past 12 Months by Age

Age Group	2011	2012	2013	2014	2015
18-29	20%	26%	28%	34%	30%
30-44	16%	18%	21%	31%	32%
45-59	8%	9%	13%	16%	20%
60+	5%	8%	7%	7%	13%
Total	12%	15%	17%	22%	24%
Number of Respondents	2,002	2,291	2,341	2,603	2,244

The Federal Reserve Consumers and Mobile Financial Services 2016

Amongst those who use their smartphones to make mobile payments, the most common reason is to pay a bill, with 65% of respondents indicating they've done this within the past 12 months [see Figure 5.4]. The next most frequent use of mobile payments, at 42%, is purchasing a physical item remotely. Interestingly, only 33% of mobile payment users have actually used their mobile phone to pay for something in a store.

Figure 5.4

Using Your Mobile Phone
Have You Done Each of the These in the Past 12 Months?

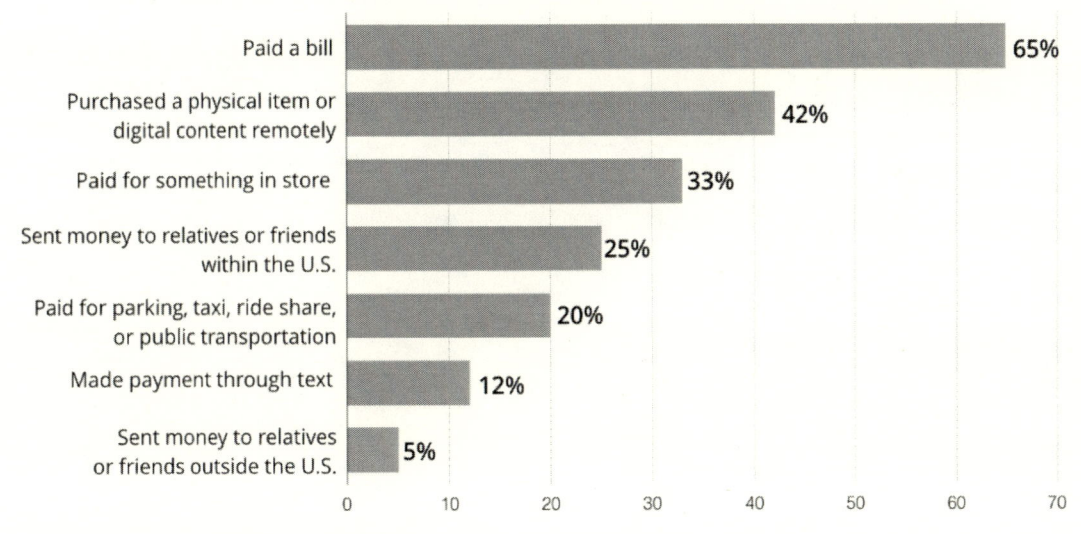

Activity	Percentage
Paid a bill	65%
Purchased a physical item or digital content remotely	42%
Paid for something in store	33%
Sent money to relatives or friends within the U.S.	25%
Paid for parking, taxi, ride share, or public transportation	20%
Made payment through text	12%
Sent money to relatives or friends outside the U.S.	5%

The Federal Reserve Consumers and Mobile Financial Services 2016

The most common form of mobile payment is made through what's known as a mobile wallet, which is simply an electronic version of a consumer wallet that offers consumers the convenience of faster transactions without having to enter credit or debit card information for each transaction. Mobile wallets replace sensitive information with randomly generated numbers—a process called tokenization—which provides greater security when making a payment, and then transmit this information using existing credit and debit card networks.

Consumers may use mobile wallets to make payments to other consumers, referred to as person-to-person, or P2P, payments, or to businesses, referred to as person-to-business, or P2B, payments, either in mobile applications, through mobile browsers, or in person at a store's point-of-sale terminal. A variety of companies provide mobile wallets, including Apple, Google, PayPal, Square, and Samsung; merchants such as Starbucks, Walmart, and CVS; and financial institutions such as JPMorgan Chase & Co. and Citibank.

Figure 5.5 highlights how frequently some of the more popular mobile wallets are used by consumers. In March of 2018, 64% of survey respondents reported they had used Venmo, which is owned by PayPal, within the past 12 months, which is up from 61% the year before. We can see that the other mobile wallets, run by tech heavyweights, come nowhere close to Venmo in terms of popularity.

Figure 5.5

Percent of Survey Respondents Using Various Mobile Payment Options Over the Last 12 Months

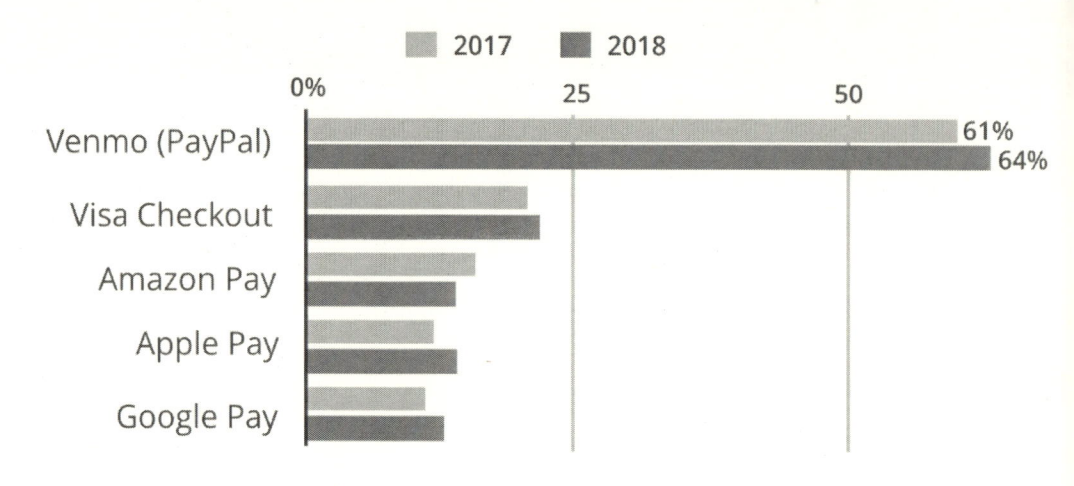

■ 2017   ■ 2018

Option	2017	2018
Venmo (PayPal)	61%	64%
Visa Checkout		
Amazon Pay		
Apple Pay		
Google Pay		

Bernstein Research: Surveys conducted in May 2017 and March 2018

One new entrant who has successfully challenged Venmo's market dominance is Zelle, which launched in 2017. Zelle is owned by a consortium of seven of the country's largest banks and is currently being used by close to twenty banks, with 70 more in the process of signing up. Given the number of banks that have integrated Zelle into their mobile app, Zelle now connects approximately half of all checking accounts in the U.S.. In 2017, $75 billion dollars passed through Zelle's network, more than double the amount that passed though Venmo.[108] Zelle's early success is another reminder that traditional financial institutions are also constantly innovating and are not just going to sit back while new FinTech firms take their market share.

All of these mobile wallets offer consumers the convenience of instant transactions without having to enter credit card information, PIN numbers, and shipping addresses each time they make a purchase. Mobile wallets also streamline the check-out time; now consumers can pay for goods by simply waving their smartphone in front of a terminal and be on their way. Mobile wallets also improve data security by replacing a consumer's payment card information with a randomly generated number or token.

Of course, one of the risks associated with mobile wallets is that consumers could lose their phone, or have it stolen. Provided the thief was able to unlock the phone, they would be free to make payments using the mobile wallet. There is also the potential for human error; for example, a consumer could accidently send money to the wrong person if they type in the wrong phone number.

There is no one law, or government agency, that oversees mobile payments. Since most of these mobile payment technologies run on legacy payment systems, such as credit and debit cards, and ACH, the laws and regulations applicable to legacy payment systems will apply to new mobile payments. For instance, Venmo uses ACH processing to fund their customer's peer-to-peer payments, therefore the laws and regulations applicable to ACH transactions apply to Venmo transactions. Determining all of the laws that apply to mobile payments depends on several factors, including agency jurisdiction, the mobile payment providers' relationship to depository institutions, and the type of account used by a consumer to make a mobile payment. If a mobile payment provider is partnering with a depository institution, federal banking regulators are authorized to examine and regulate the mobile payment provider and the service it is offering.

In the U.S., states have licensing and regulatory authority over businesses that provide money transfer services or payment instruments, and this can include mobile payment providers. So FinTech firms such as PayPal and Google Pay are subject to state money transmitter laws. Also, any firm that transmit moneys, whether they use traditional or FinTech products, are subject to federal anti-money laundering laws.

Nonbank mobile payment providers may also be subject to Consumer Financial Protection Bureau and Federal Trade Commission consumer protection enforcement actions as these two agencies share joint enforcement jurisdiction over certain nonbank providers of financial products and services. In fact, the FTC has brought and settled enforcement actions alleging unfair or deceptive conduct by several wireless providers of mobile payment services. In addition, any mobile payment product that includes wireless bill charges as a payment method may be subject to the Federal Communications Commission authority as they have jurisdiction over wireless providers.

Finally, consumer protection laws, such as the Electronic Fund Transfer Act, which apply to traditional funding sources, do not yet cover payments funded by mobile wallet balances or mobile carrier billing. To address this gap, in October 2016, the CFPB issued a final rule to add prepaid cards and some of the payment services that FinTech providers are offering, such as PayPal, to the definition of accounts covered under regulations applicable to electronic fund transfer systems, such as automated teller machine transfers, telephone bill-payment services, point-of-sale terminal transfers in stores, and preauthorized transfers from or to a consumer's account (such as direct deposit and Social Security payments). The rule would extend protections for error resolution and liability for unauthorized transfers to prepaid account and mobile wallet balances, but the effective date of the rule has been postponed to April 1, 2019.[109]

Decentralized Payments

While many new mobile payment technologies utilize longstanding payments infrastructure, such as ACH or credit card networks, there is an entirely new method of sending value utilizing distributed ledger and blockchain technology that does not fit neatly within existing payment legal frameworks. Blockchain technology has the potential to fundamentally alter how money changes hands around the world. Through blockchain and other forms of distributed ledger technology, a payment system can operate across a distributed network of computers without the need for intermediaries such as banks. This could reduce costs dramatically. One global investment fund suggests that distributed ledger technology could reduce banks' infrastructure costs attributable to cross-border payments, securities trading, and regulatory compliance by between $15-20 billion per year by 2022.[110]

Thus far, most payment developments utilizing cryptocurrencies and distributed ledger technology have been focused on the retail, or consumer, sector. But as cryptocurrencies are viewed less as stores of value and more as means of reducing friction within the payments process, expect to see new developments related to wholesale payments.[6] Right now, a range of wholesale payment solutions are being developed that build upon the Bitcoin infrastructure, and there is also a range of alternative digital currencies either available or soon to be launched, known as "altcoins," that more specifically target opportunities in the wholesale payments market.

The regulations governing U.S. payment systems were designed for a bank-based system. Therefore, none of the federal statutes or regulations that apply to traditional payment systems contain explicit language about their applicability, or non-applicability, to decentralized payment systems. Adding to the confusion is that for some of these decentralized systems, there may not be a single entity that owns or operates the system and can therefore be held accountable. Ripple provides an excellent example of this phenomenon. Ripple is an open-source Internet software that enables users to conduct payments across national boundaries in multiple currencies. Through the Ripple Protocol, peer-to-peer transactions are settled across a decentralized network of computers. As a result, Ripple circumvents many of the fees and reduces many of the risks involved in interbank funds transfers, particularly in international transactions. Software is embedded within the Ripple protocol that governs how users' computers interact with each other, but the protocol does not affect users' legal rights and obligations and unlike other digital currency protocols, the Ripple Protocol is currency agnostic and users are not required to transact in the Protocol's native currency, XRP.

---

[6] Recall that wholesale payments are large value, time critical, payments that are typically sent by banks.

Because Ripple's primary customer base is financial institutions, regulators thus far treat Ripple as a third-party vendor to financial institutions. But because of its decentralized nature, it may not make sense to regulate it as if it were software that financial institutions simply install. Thus, Ripple currently sits in a regulatory grey area.[111]

While Ripple holds the promise of utilizing distributed ledger technology to facilitate real-time, low-fee, cross-border payments, we have yet to see a large-scale deployment of the technology in the marketplace. In March 2018, the Society for Worldwide Interbank Financial Telecommunications (SWIFT), which is used by banks and other financial institutions to securely send and receive information such as money transfer instructions, concluded a proof of concept that used blockchain technology to reconcile international payments between the accounts of 34 banks.[112] While the proof of concept met all the technical requirements, SWIFT found that further progress is needed on the distributed ledger technology itself before it will be ready to support production-grade applications in large-scale, mission-critical global infrastructures.

Several other blockchain tests started by the financial industry over the past few years have been recently shelved, including projects launched by the post-trade financial services company Depository Trust & Clearing Corporation and global bank BNP Paribas.[113] Despite these setbacks, other blockchain projects are moving forward, such as Quorum, which is an open-source blockchain platform developed by JP Morgan to be used for business processes. In fact, JP Morgan is considering spinning off Quorum as a separate company because the technology has attracted significant outside interest.[114]

There are countless other blockchain projects and business solutions currently in use and more are being deployed every day. These include use cases related to: supply chain management, digital identity, land titles, trade finance, commodity exchanges, decentralized electricity, and additive manufacturing. Despite its halting progress to date, blockchain and distributed ledger technology is expected to be an integral part of payment and other business systems for decades to come.

A Push for Faster Payments in the U.S.

This book's primary focus is on U.S. FinTech developments, but when it comes to payments, many other countries have already upgraded their payment systems to take advantage of improvements in technology, allowing payments to be sent within seconds between payers and recipients. While traditional noncash payment methods in the U.S. provide a platform for consumers and businesses to send payments between almost any bank account, these systems are not designed to complete a payment transaction from end to end at the level of speed consumer's desire. While a number of new innovative payment solutions that are being developed in the U.S. that can facilitate faster settlement, the problem, from a public policy perspective, is that these new FinTech payment methods do not permit seamless payments between all consumers and businesses with interoperability in various solutions.

In most countries where faster payments have been implemented, the payments industry was initially driven to design a faster payment system as a result of a government mandate or regulation. But unlike many other countries that have implemented real-time payment systems, the United States does not have a single central authority to mandate payment standards and improvements across the industry as a whole. Adding to the challenge is the fact that most countries that have implemented faster payments were able to establish a solution allowing providers to build on top of a single platform. But the U.S. has several platforms, and with over 10,000 depository institutions and hundreds of nonbank payment providers, it is more challenging to implement improvements to the U.S. payments infrastructures in a coordinated way.

To help overcome these challenges, in 2015, the Federal Reserve convened the Faster Payments Task Force, consisting of financial institutions, nonbank providers, businesses, retailers, consumer groups, standards bodies, and other organizations involved in making, receiving, and processing payments.[115] The task force's mission was to "identify and evaluate alternative approaches for implementing safe, ubiquitous, faster payments capabilities in the United States."

In early 2016, the task force solicited proposals for end-to-end faster payments solutions that could meet their criteria. Specifically, they were looking for solutions that: could initiate and/or receive payments to and from any entity; provided a straightforward, simple, and reliable end-user experience; and contained the ability for end users to make payments anytime, anywhere, using a variety of access channels. The taskforce received and provided feedback on a number of proposals representing a broad universe of creative and innovative ways to deliver faster payments, including solutions that work in similar ways to those in the market today, as well as conceptual solutions that would leverage the latest, most cutting-edge thinking and technology. Some proposals were structured like legacy payment systems that use a centralized clearing and settlement mechanism while others focused on distributed networks. Some proposals were based on traditional assets held in transaction accounts, while others depended on new asset forms like digital currencies.

In July 2017, the Faster Payments Task Force released their final report that indicated how well each proposal met their criteria while also including a number of recommendations.[116] Because U.S. regulators cannot mandate a single solution, the task force is pushing a market-driven approach to payment system innovation. This approach relies on multiple solution operators and other stakeholders voluntarily collaborating. The problem of course is how do you achieve broad adoption? A large population of consumers, businesses, and government agencies will need to have knowledge of, access to, and the motivation to use faster payments. The payment providers need incentives to develop a solution that meets the task force's criteria and can interoperate with competing solutions. All of these stakeholders have their own unique motivations and incentives and without a government mandate, it's uncertain if the U.S. will be able to catch-up to other countries in terms of payments technology.

Chapter 6: FinTech Wealth Management and Financial Account Aggregators

FinTech Wealth Management

The wealth management industry is massive and has historically been very profitable. PwC estimates that at the end of 2016, the amount of assets under management by wealth management firms around the world was approximately 85 trillion dollars.[117] The industry has traditionally been labor-intensive, with scores of advisers and retail brokers across the country meeting with clients face-to-face on a periodic basis. Given the industry's size and lack of technological sophistication, it is no wonder tech startups have begun to put their own spin on the very old business of managing other people's money. These new FinTech firms, commonly called robo-advisors, provide automated, algorithm-driven financial planning services based on investors' data and risk preferences. Some robo-advisors provide investment advice directly to the client with limited, if any, direct human interaction with investment advisory personnel. While other robo-advisors provide advice by having investment advisory personnel use the interactive platform to generate an investment plan that is discussed and refined with the client.

It is estimated that robo-advisory firms currently hold $200 billion dollars in assets under management, with that amount expected to grow dramatically over the next few years.[118] One research firm estimates that robo-advisory firms will have as much as $1 trillion dollars in assets under management by 2020 and as much as $4 trillion by 2022.[119] Some of the more prominent robo-advisors include Betterment, Personal Capital, and Wealthfront.

The process of investing with a robo-advisor all begins when the customer goes to the robo-advisor's website and enters in personal information, such as their: age, income, investing goals, risk tolerance, investing timeframe, and their current financial assets. Information pertaining to the investors risk tolerance is often obtained through the use of a questionnaire designed to identify each investor's willingness and ability to take risk. Once this information is collected, it is fed into the robo-advisor's proprietary algorithm which then spits out one or more recommended investing strategies for the client. Once the customer selects their preferred strategy, the platform will automatically execute trades and periodically rebalance the customer's portfolio in response to the performance of the portfolio assets and the customer's goals. Finally, the customer is free to periodically adjust the information they originally provided should their financial circumstances or risk tolerance change. The platform will adjust the investor's portfolio accordingly.

Robo-advisors are growing in popularity for several reasons. For starters, they are cheaper than traditional financial advisers who typically charge each client an annual fee anywhere between 1% and 2% of client assets under management. In contrast, robo-advisors charge between 0.15% and 0.5% in management fees. Customers are also flocking to robo-advisors because they offer the same, or higher, performance as traditional advisors. According to the Financial Times and CNBC, between 80% and 90% of active managers underperform their stated benchmark over a period of 10 to 15 years.[120] Why pay active managers if they perform worse than the market? By utilizing passive investment strategies, robo-advisors can beat active managers, providing higher returns to their customers at a lower price. Finally, robo-advisors are attracting customers who do not meet the minimum net worth requirements that most traditional wealth management firms require. Many robo-advisors don't require a minimum amount to invest, allowing more people to use their services and to take on less financial risk.

As with any type of financial advice, whether it's provided by a robo-advisor or traditional financial adviser, consumers face risks of receiving unsuitable investment advice. While a human adviser may be able to mitigate this risk by probing consumers for more information to assess needs, risk tolerance, or other important factors, a robo-advisor's ability to mitigate this risk may be based on a discrete set of questions to develop a customer profile. Financial advisers of all kinds can also make inaccurate or inappropriate economic assumptions, perhaps due to a failure to factor in changing economic conditions, which could result in flawed investment recommendations. While human advisers may be able to mitigate this risk to some degree based on their ability to adjust to economic conditions, a robo-advisor's ability to mitigate this risk is based on whether its algorithm has been updated to reflect the most recent economic conditions.

Robo-advisory firms can be investment advisors or broker dealers, both of which employ licensed professionals to assist investors with their financial goals. Brokers are paid through commissions for the trades they make on behalf of their clients and are governed by Financial Industry Regulatory Authority (FINRA) rules. FINRA is a self-regulatory organization that regulates member brokerage firms and exchange markets. Investment advisors are paid either a straight fee for their time or a percentage of the assets under management and are governed by Securities and Exchange Commission rules. Many FINRA registered broker-dealers are also registered as investment advisers.

Investment advisers are held to a higher legal standard than brokers. Specifically, investment advisors owe a fiduciary duty to their clients, which requires advisors act in the best interests of their clients and put their clients' interests above their own. Brokers, on the other hand, are held to a suitability standard, which means that as long as an investment recommendation meets a client's defined need and objective, it is deemed appropriate.

In 2016, the Department of Labor proposed the so-called "fiduciary rule," which automatically elevated all financial professionals who work with retirement plans or provide retirement planning advice to the level of a fiduciary.[121] The rule would effectively hold brokers to the same standard that is currently applied to investment advisers. The fiduciary rule has been controversial from the beginning and has gone through a lengthy legal challenge. The Department of Labor is currently not enforcing the rule and it's unlikely it ever will.[122] But this does not mean broker-dealers are entirely off the hook. In April of 2018, the SEC released a proposed rule that establishes a new "best interest" standard of conduct for broker-dealers when recommending a securities transaction or investment strategy to a retail customer, including that the broker-dealer act without placing its own interests ahead of the retail customer's interests, and disclose and mitigate certain conflicts of interest.[123] If this rule is finalized, it would significantly close the gap between the fiduciary standard that is currently applied to investment advisers and the current suitability standard that applies to brokers.

Under the Investment Advisers Act of 1940 and state securities laws, any entity or individual that offers investment advice for compensation generally must register as an investment adviser—with the SEC or the states—and adhere to various reporting and conduct requirements.[124] Robo-advisers offering wealth management advice would generally be subject to the same federal and state oversight as traditional investment advisers and customers of robo-advisors receive the same protections as those of traditional advisers.

As mentioned, when providing advice, investment advisers—traditional or FinTech—are considered fiduciaries to their clients, which means they owe a duty of care and loyalty to their clients, and they must disclose all actual or potential conflicts of interest, and act in their clients' best interest. Recognizing that robo-advisors utilize a unique delivery mechanism compared to traditional advisers, the SEC issued guidance to robo-advisors in 2017 that offered suggestions for how they can meet their obligations under the Investment Advisers Act.[125] This includes suggestions on the substance and presentation of disclosures, the provision of suitable advice, and effective compliance programs.

For the substance and presentation of disclosures, an investment adviser has a duty to make full and fair disclosure of all material facts, and to employ reasonable care to avoid misleading clients. This information must be sufficiently specific so that a client is able to understand the investment adviser's business practices and conflicts of interests. Because most robo-advisers interact with their clients solely online, with limited human involvement, they need to think critically about how they communicate this information electronically. The SEC notes that robo-advisers (like all registered investment advisers) need to disclose information regarding their particular business practices and related risks, which includes a description of the algorithmic functions used to manage client accounts and the assumptions and limitations behind the algorithm. These disclosures should be made prior to the sign-up process and be easy to understand. For the provision of suitable advice, all investment advisers must make a reasonable determination that the investment advice provided is suitable for the client based on the client's financial situation and investment objectives. Robo-advisers typically acquire this information through the use of a questionnaire, and the SEC recommends the following factors be considered when designing the questionnaire: whether the questions elicit sufficient information to allow the robo-advisor to conclude that its initial recommendations and ongoing investment advice are suitable and appropriate for that client based on his or her financial situation and investment objective; whether the questions in the questionnaire are sufficiently clear; and whether steps have been taken to address inconsistent client responses. Finally, the SEC's guidance notes that each registered investment adviser is required to establish an internal compliance program that addresses the adviser's performance of its fiduciary and substantive obligations under the Investment Advisers Act. Robo-advisers should incorporate the unique aspects of their business model into their compliance program. For example, a robo-advisor's reliance on algorithms, the limited, if any, human interaction with clients, and the provision of advisory services over the Internet may create or accentuate risk exposures that should be addressed through written policies and procedures.

Similar to the SEC, FINRA recognized that many of the broker-dealers it supervised were beginning to adopt digital investment advice tools, so in 2016, they issued a report reminding broker-dealers of their obligations under FINRA rules and sharing effective practices related to digital investment advice, including with respect to technology management, portfolio development and conflicts of interest mitigation.[126] The FINRA report on robo-advisors focused on the governance and supervision of investment recommendations in two areas: first, the algorithms that drive digital investment tools; and second, the construction of client portfolios, including potential conflicts of interest that may arise in those portfolios. FINRA recommends that robo-advisors should be able to answer the following questions about their algorithms: 1) Are the methodologies tested by independent third-parties? 2) Can the firm explain to regulators how the tool works and how it complies with regulatory requirements? And 3) Is there exception reporting to identify situations where a tool's output deviates from what might be expected and, if so, what are the parameters that trigger such reporting? FINRA also encourages robo-advisors to have governance and supervision structures in place to review both the customer profiles and pre-packaged portfolios that may be offered to clients.

Robo-advisers are examined just like traditional advisers. In its 2018, National Exam Program Examination Priorities document, the SEC noted that it will continue to examine investment advisers—including robo-advisors—that offer investment advice through automated or digital platforms.[127] These Examinations will focus on registrants' compliance programs, including oversight of computer program algorithms that generate recommendations, marketing materials, investor data protection, and disclosure of conflicts of interest.

Finally, know that state regulators are responsible for conducting examinations of investment advisers that operate in fewer than 15 states and hold client assets under management of less than $100 million dollars. However, as of the end of 2017, no robo-advisor met these criteria and was therefore regulated solely by the states.

Financial Account Aggregators

As the name implies, financial account aggregators allow consumers to aggregate the information from their various financial accounts, including their assets in bank accounts and brokerage accounts, to enable them to better see their financial health and receive advice on alternative ways to save money or manage their finances. Account aggregators allow consumers to access this information either online or on mobile devises, and some of the more well-known firms providing this service include Mint and HelloWallet.

While account aggregators certainly provide a convenient service, they also pose unique risks that consumers should be aware of. The main risk is that consumers could potentially be more exposed to losses due to fraud. If a consumer authorizes an account aggregator to access their financial accounts and grants the aggregator authority to make transfers, the consumer may be liable for fraudulent transfers made. Market participants do not agree about whether consumers using account aggregators will be reimbursed if they experience fraudulent losses in their financial accounts. Some banks have even stated publicly that they may not reimburse losses from consumer accounts if the consumer provided his or her account credentials to an account aggregator and fraudulent activity subsequently occurs in the consumer's account.[128] The relevant regulatory agencies don't see eye to eye on this issue either. In 2017, the Consumer Financial Protection Bureau issued non-binding guidance which stated that Consumers should have reasonable and practical means to dispute and resolve instances of unauthorized transactions.[129] The Federal Reserve on the other hand, has suggested that industry stakeholders will need to come to agreement on which party bears responsibility for unauthorized transactions.[130]

Another risk associated with account aggregators is that some firms may hold consumer data without disclosing what rights consumers have to delete the data or prevent the data from being shared with other parties. However, the Gramm-Leach-Bliley Act of 1999 generally requires FinTech firms and traditional financial institutions to safeguard nonpublic personal information about customers.

Because of these risks, several large banks have intervened at times to limit the flow of information to some account aggregator websites. This occurred in late 2015, when several big banks including JPMorgan Chase, Bank of America and Wells Fargo expressed concern that the aggregator sites could threaten consumers' account security and that these services overload bank websites at busy times by requesting updated information about consumer accounts from bank servers.[131] While these concerns may be valid, it's important to keep in mind that banks also have a competitive incentive not to share their customer's data with tech-savvy FinTech firms who could potentially utilize the data to provide superior products or services.

To address some of these issues, several financial institutions have negotiated contractual arrangements with individual account aggregators. For instance, in 2017, JPMorgan Chase and Intuit, which owns Mint.com, TurboTax and QuickBooks, reached an agreement to allow Chase customers to check account information on the technology firm's sites without sharing their Chase passwords.[132] To do this, Chase customers authorize the bank to electronically share their financial information with Intuit's financial-management sites, and the data is shared via an application-programming interface, or API. This eliminates the old process whereby customers had to manually enter their Chase passwords into the sites. As part of the agreement, Intuit agreed not to sell customer data to third-parties, which has been a concern of many banks.

As more and more consumers continue to enjoy and demand the convenience provided by account aggregators, expect to see similar types of agreements between aggregators and banks to become commonplace.

Acknowledgements

This book arose from an online course I developed by the same name: "FinTech Law and Policy." As I was developing scripts to record for the course lectures, I realized that I had accumulated a significant amount of material that could be packaged into a book. Neither the online course, nor the book, would have been possible were it not for the excellent work of several people. Ryan Clements helped me with much of the material in this book and is an expert in FinTech Law in his own right. Tara Kramling from Duke's Learning Innovation office was the project manager for the online course and did an exceptional job shepherding the project from start to finish. Nicholas Janes developed some amazing graphics for the course and put together all the charts for the course and this book. Mich Donovan did a fantastic job filming and editing the videos for the course. They are all exceptional talents and I am thankful to them.

References

[1] Arner, Douglas W. and Barberis, Janos Nathan and Buckley, Ross P., The Evolution of Fintech: A New Post-Crisis Paradigm? (October 1, 2015). University of Hong Kong Faculty of Law Research Paper No. 2015/047; UNSW Law Research Paper No. 2016-62. Available at SSRN: https://ssrn.com/abstract=2676553 or http://dx.doi.org/10.2139/ssrn.2676553

[2] Dimon, Jamie. Dear Fellow Shareholders, - JPMorgan Chase. JPMorgan Chase, 4 Apr. 2017, https://www.jpmorganchase.com/corporate/investor-relations/document/ar2016-ceolettershareholders.pdf

[3] Smith, Aaron. "Record Shares of Americans Now Own Smartphones, Have Home Broadband." Pew Research Center, Pew Research Center, 12 Jan. 2017, www.pewresearch.org/fact-tank/2017/01/12/evolution-of-technology/.

[4] Stephanie Barello. "Consumer spending and U.S. employment from the 2007–2009 recession through 2022," Monthly Labor Review, U.S. Bureau of Labor Statistics, October 2014, https://doi.org/10.21916/mlr.2014.34.

[5] GSS Data Explorer | NORC at the University of Chicago, gssdataexplorer.norc.org/variables/448/vshow.

[6] Harmon, Florence E. "UNITED STATES OF AMERICA Before the SECURITIES AND EXCHANGE COMMISSION." Ww.sec.gov, 4 Nov. 2008, www.sec.gov/litigation/admin/2008/33-8984.pdf.

[7] Horigan, Jacqueline. "Division of Banks Announces $2 Million Settlement Over Unlicensed Loan Servicing and Lending Activities at LendingClub Corporation." Mass.gov, 2 Apr. 2018, www.mass.gov/news/division-of-banks-announces-2-million-settlement-over-unlicensed-loan-servicing-and-lending.

[8] Cotney, David J. "LendingClub Corporation." Mass.gov, 1 June 2011, www.mass.gov/consent-order/lendingclub-corporation.

[9] Randles, Jonathan. "PayPal to To Pay $7.7M To Settle Sanctions Violations - Law360." Law360 - The Newswire for Business Lawyers, Law360, 25 Mar. 2015, www.law360.com/articles/635728?scroll=1.

[10] Calvery, Jennifer Shaskey. "UNITED STATES OF AMERICA DEPARTMENT OF THE ... - FinCEN.gov." Fincen.gov, 5 May 2015, https://www.fincen.gov/sites/default/files/shared/Ripple_Assessment.pdf

[11] "Bitcoin Exchangers Plead Guilty In Manhattan Federal Court In Connection With The Sale Of Approximately $1 Million In Bitcoins For Use On The Silk Road Website." The United States Department of Justice, 4 Sept. 2014, www.justice.gov/usao-sdny/pr/bitcoin-exchangers-plead-guilty-manhattan-federal-court-connection-sale-approximately-1.

[12] Kirkpatrick, Christopher J. UNITED STATES OF AMERICA Before the COMMODITY FUTURES TRADING COMMISSION. 17 Sept. 2015, https://www.cftc.gov/sites/default/files/idc/groups/public/@lrenforcementactions/documents/legalpleading/enfcoinfliprorder09172015.pdf

[13] "SEC Charges Former Bitcoin-Denominated Exchange and Operator With Fraud." SEC.gov, 21 Feb. 2018, www.sec.gov/news/press-release/2018-23.

[14] "SEC Halts Alleged Initial Coin Offering Scam." SEC.gov, 30 Jan. 2018, www.sec.gov/news/press-release/2018-8.

[15] Fields, Brent J. "UNITED STATES OF AMERICA before the SECURITIES AND EXCHANGE COMMISSION." SEC.GOV, 11 Dec. 2017, www.sec.gov/litigation/admin/2017/33-10445.pdf.

[16] "FINANCIAL TECHNOLOGY Additional Steps by Regulators Could Better Protect Consumers and Aid Regulatory Oversight." GOA.GOV, Mar. 2018, www.gao.gov/assets/700/690803.pdf.

[17] Yazdani, Dariush, and Grégory Weber. "Redrawing the Lines: FinTech's Growing Influence on Financial Services." Global FinTech Report 2017, 2017, www.pwc.com/gx/en/industries/financial-services/assets/pwc-global-fintech-report-2017.pdf.
[18] "Project Catalyst." Consumer Financial Protection Bureau, www.consumerfinance.gov/about-us/project-catalyst/.
[19] "Lab CFTC." U.S. COMMODITY FUTURES TRADING COMMISSION, www.cftc.gov/LabCFTC/index.htm.
[20] "Responsible Innovation." OCC: Truth in Lending, 3 Mar. 2017, www.occ.gov/topics/responsible-innovation/index-innovation.html.
[21] Federal Reserve Bank of Boston. "Mobile Payments Industry Workgroup." Federal Reserve Bank of Boston, 17 Nov. 2017, www.bostonfed.org/about-the-boston-fed/business-areas/payment-strategies/mobile-payments-industry-workgroup.aspx.
[22] "U.S. Department of the Treasury." Ukraine-/Russia-Related Designations and Identification Update; Syria Designations; Kingpin Act Designations; Issuance of Ukraine-/Russia-Related General Licenses 12 and 13; Publication of New FAQs and Updated FAQ, 1 Dec. 2016, www.treasury.gov/press-center/press-releases/Pages/jl0676.aspx.
[23] "FINANCIAL TECHNOLOGY Additional Steps by Regulators Could Better Protect Consumers and Aid Regulatory Oversight." GOA.GOV, Mar. 2018, www.gao.gov/assets/700/690803.pdf.

[24] Regulatory Sandbox. Financial Conduct Authority, Nov. 2015, https://www.fca.org.uk/publication/research/regulatory-sandbox.pdf.
[25] "CFPB Announces First No-Action Letter to Upstart Network." Consumer Financial Protection Bureau, Sept. 14AD, 2017, www.consumerfinance.gov/about-us/newsroom/cfpb-announces-first-no-action-letter-upstart-network/.
[26] Stanley, Aaron. "Arizona Becomes First U.S. State To Launch Regulatory Sandbox For Fintech." Forbes, Forbes Magazine, 24 Mar. 2018, www.forbes.com/sites/astanley/2018/03/23/arizona-becomes-first-u-s-state-to-launch-regulatory-sandbox-for-fintech/#537c80f61372.
[27] "Arizona Becomes First State in U.S. to Offer Fintech Regulatory Sandbox." Azag.gov, Mark Brnovich, 23 Mar. 2018, www.azag.gov/press-release/arizona-becomes-first-state-us-offer-fintech-regulatory-sandbox.
[28] "Market Structure, Business Models and Financial Stability Implications ." BIS.ORG, Committee on the Global Financial System (CGFS) and the Financial Stability Board (FSB), 22 May 2017, www.bis.org/publ/cgfs_fsb1.pdf.
[29] Federal Reserve Bank of Boston. "U.S. Consumers' Awareness and Use of Marketplace Lending." Federal Reserve Bank of Boston, 8 Jan. 2018, www.bostonfed.org/publications/current-policy-perspectives/2017/us-consumers-awareness-and-use-of-marketplace-lending.aspx.
[30] "MARQUETTE NAT. BANK v. FIRST OF OMAHA CORP." Findlaw, caselaw.findlaw.com/us-supreme-court/439/299.html.
[31] Examination Guidance for Third-Party Lending. FDIC.GOV, 29 July 2016, www.fdic.gov/news/news/financial/2016/fil16050a.pdf.
[32] Rudegeair, Peter. "LendingClub CEO Fired Over Faulty Loans." The Wall Street Journal, Dow Jones & Company, 9 May 2016, www.wsj.com/articles/lendingclub-ceo-resigns-over-sales-review-1462795070.
[33] "Madden v. Midland Funding, LLC, No. 14-2131 (2d Cir. 2015)." Justia Law, law.justia.com/cases/federal/appellate-courts/ca2/14-2131/14-2131-2015-05-22.html.
[34] Enloe, Caren. "Madden Fix Bill Passes House, Faces Uncertain Fate in Senate." Lexology, Lexology, 5 Mar. 2018, www.lexology.com/library/detail.aspx?g=064e23c2-618d-42a7-8e02-b0bf4ffdfeeb.
[35] "OCC Issues Responsible Innovation Framework." OCC: Truth in Lending, 26 Oct. 2016,

www.occ.gov/news-issuances/news-releases/2016/nr-occ-2016-135.html.

[36] Remarks By Thomas J. Curry Comptroller of the Currency Regarding Special Purpose National Bank Charters for Fintech Companies. Georgetown University Law Center, 2 Dec. 2016, www.occ.treas.gov/news-issuances/speeches/2016/pub-speech-2016-152.pdf.

[37] Evaluating Charter Applications From Financial Technology Companies. The Office of the Comptroller of the Currency, Mar. 2017, occ.gov/publications/publications-by-type/licensing-manuals/file-pub-lm-fintech-licensing-manual-supplement.pdf.

[38] Freifeld, Karen. "Judge Tosses NY Lawsuit over National Charters for Online Lenders." Reuters, Thomson Reuters, 12 Dec. 2017, www.reuters.com/article/us-new-york-occ-fintech/judge-tosses-ny-lawsuit-over-national-charters-for-online-lenders-idUSKBN1E62UD.

[39] "July 2007 Regional Economist | St. Louis Fed." Federal Reserve Bank of St. Louis, Federal Reserve Bank of St. Louis, www.stlouisfed.org/publications/regional-economist/july-2007.

[40] Dash, Eric. "Wal-Mart Abandons Bank Plans." The New York Times, The New York Times, 17 Mar. 2007, www.nytimes.com/2007/03/17/business/17bank.html.

[41] Lawler, Ryan. "SoFi Has Applied for a Bank Charter." TechCrunch, TechCrunch, 12 June 2017, techcrunch.com/2017/06/12/sofi-applies-to-be-a-bank/.

[42] Irrera, Anna. "SoFi Withdraws U.S. Banking Application, Citing Leadership Change." Reuters, Thomson Reuters, 13 Oct. 2017, www.reuters.com/article/us-sofi-future/sofi-withdraws-u-s-banking-application-citing-leadership-change-idUSKBN1CI2XC.

[43] Rudegeair, Peter. "Jack Dorsey's Square Makes a Move Into Banking." The Wall Street Journal, Dow Jones & Company, 6 Sept. 2017, www.wsj.com/articles/jack-dorseys-square-makes-a-move-into-banking-1504737851.

[44] Witkowski, Rachel. "Square quietly withdraws bank application." *American Banker.* https://www.americanbanker.com/news/square-quietly-withdraws-bank-application

[45] Lawler, Ryan. "Mobile Banking Startup Varo Money Has Applied for a Bank Charter." TechCrunch, TechCrunch, 25 July 2017, techcrunch.com/2017/07/25/varo-money-applies-for-bank-charter/.

[46] Leger, Donna Leinwand. "How FBI Brought down Cyber-Underworld Site Silk Road." USA Today, Gannett Satellite Information Network, 15 May 2014, www.usatoday.com/story/news/nation/2013/10/21/fbi-cracks-silk-road/2984921/.

[47] Pollock, Darryn. "The Mess That Was Mt. Gox: Four Years On." Cointelegraph, Cointelegraph, 23 June 2018, cointelegraph.com/news/the-mess-that-was-mt-gox-four-years-on.

[48] "The Coincheck Cryptocurrency Hack: Everything You Need to Know." Fortune, Fortune, fortune.com/2018/01/29/coincheck-japan-nem-hack/.

[49] "All Cryptocurrencies." www.investing.com/crypto/currencies.

[50] "Choose Your Bitcoin Wallet." Bitcoin - Open Source P2P Money, bitcoin.org/en/choose-your-wallet.

[51] See Tali Arbel, *Why Bitcoin is the HBO hackers' payment of choice,* Business News Network (August 8, 2017), http://www.bnn.ca/why-bitcoin-is-the-hbo-hackers-payment-of-choice-1.824819.

[52] Alexander, Harriet. "Idaho Teenager Becomes Millionaire by Investing $1,000 Gift in Bitcoin - and Wins Bet with His Parents." The Telegraph, Telegraph Media Group, 24 June 2017, www.telegraph.co.uk/news/2017/06/24/idaho-teenager-became-millionaire-investing-1000-gift-bitcoin/.

[53] Bishop, Jordan. "Meet The Man Traveling The World On $25 Million Of Bitcoin Profits." Forbes, Forbes Magazine, 7 July 2017, www.forbes.com/sites/bishopjordan/2017/07/07/bitcoin-millionaire/#305e00166261.

[54] Hale, Galina, et al. "How Futures Trading Changed Bitcoin Prices." Federal Reserve Bank of San Francisco, Federal Reserve Bank of San Francisco, 7 May 2018, www.frbsf.org/economic-

research/publications/economic-letter/2018/may/how-futures-trading-changed-bitcoin-prices/.
[55] Bank Secrecy Act Regulations – Definitions and Other Regulations Relating to Money Services Businesses, 76 FR 43585 (July 21, 2011)

[56] "FinCEN Issues Guidance on Virtual Currencies and Regulatory Responsibilities." USA PATRIOT Act | FinCEN.gov, www.fincen.gov/news/news-releases/fincen-issues-guidance-virtual-currencies-and-regulatory-responsibilities.

[57] Calvery, Jennifer Shaskey. "UNITED STATES OF AMERICA DEPARTMENT OF THE ... - FinCEN.gov." Fincen.gov, 5 May 2015, https://www.fincen.gov/sites/default/files/shared/Ripple_Assessment.pdf

[58] Hudock, Steve. "FinCEN Fines Ripple Labs Inc. in First Civil Enforcement Action Against a Virtual Currency Exchanger." USA PATRIOT Act | FinCEN.gov, 5 May 2015, www.fincen.gov/news/news-releases/fincen-fines-ripple-labs-inc-first-civil-enforcement-action-against-virtual.

[59] "State-by-State Regulatory Tracker for Digital Currency Policy." Coin Center, 23 Aug. 2017, coincenter.org/page/state-digital-currency-regulatory-tracker.

[60] Osipovich, Alexander. "Can the Biggest U.S. Bitcoin Exchange Win Over Wall Street?" The Wall Street Journal, Dow Jones & Company, 27 May 2018, www.wsj.com/articles/can-the-biggest-u-s-bitcoin-exchange-win-over-wall-street-1527418800?utm_campaign=morning scan plus-may 29 2018&utm_medium=email&utm_source=newsletter&eid=a7448dba84c0e8c1ebedfe4d04948d35&bxid=57c83f5815dd96977d8b4af9.

[61] United States, Congress, "BitLicense Regulatory Framework." BitLicense Regulatory Framework, New York State. www.dfs.ny.gov/legal/regulations/bitlicense_reg_framework.htm.

[62] UNIFORM REGULATION OF VIRTUAL-CURRENCY BUSINESSES ACT. NATIONAL CONFERENCE OF COMMISSIONERS ON UNIFORM STATE LAWS, 9 Oct. 2017, www.uniformlaws.org/shared/docs/regulation of virtual currencies/URVCBA_Final_2017oct9.pdf.

[63] UNITED STATES OF AMERICA Before the COMMODITY FUTURES TRADING COMMISSION. The Commodity Futures Trading Commission, 17 Sept. 2015, www.cftc.gov/sites/default/files/idc/groups/public/@lrenforcementactions/documents/legalpleading/enfcoinfliprorder09172015.pdf.

[64] United States, Congress, Federal Reserve System. "Regulation CC (Availability of Funds and Collection of Checks)." Regulation CC (Availability of Funds and Collection of Checks), 28 Feb. 2017. www.federalreserve.gov/paymentsystems/regcc-about.htm.

[65] "CFTC Issues Proposed Interpretation on Virtual Currency 'Actual Delivery' in Retail Transactions." U.S. COMMODITY FUTURES TRADING COMMISSION, www.cftc.gov/PressRoom/PressReleases/7664-17.

[66] "For Bitcoin Futures, the CFTC Defends the Indefensible." The Alcohol Pharmacology Education Partnership, Biopiracy in the Amazon, 5 Jan. 2018, sites.duke.edu/thefinregblog/2018/01/04/for-bitcoin-futures-the-cftc-defends-the-indefensible/.

[67] CFTC Backgrounder on Self-Certified Contracts for Bitcoin Products. U.S. COMMODITY FUTURES TRADING COMMISSION, 1 Dec. 2017, www.cftc.gov/sites/default/files/idc/groups/public/@newsroom/documents/file/bitcoin_factsheet120117.pdf.

[68] SECURITIES AND EXCHANGE COMMISSION. Bats BZX Exchange, 10 Mar. 2017, www.sec.gov/rules/sro/batsbzx/2017/34-80206.pdf.

[69] "Staff Letter: Engaging on Fund Innovation and Cryptocurrency-Related Holdings." SEC.gov, 18 Jan. 2018, www.sec.gov/divisions/investment/noaction/2018/cryptocurrency-011818.html.

[70] "SPEECHES & TESTIMONY." U.S. COMMODITY FUTURES TRADING COMMISSION, www.cftc.gov/PressRoom/SpeechesTestimony/opaquintenz8.

[71] Winklevoss, Cameron. "A Proposal for a Self-Regulatory Organization for the U.S. Virtual Currency Industry." Medium, Augmenting Humanity, 13 Mar. 2018, medium.com/gemini/a-

proposal-for-a-self-regulatory-organization-for-the-u-s-virtual-currency-industry-79e4d7891cfc.
[72] "Internal Revenue Bulletin: 2014-16." Internal Revenue Service, 14 Apr. 2014, www.irs.gov/irb/2014-16_IRB.
[73] Schweikert, and David. "Text - H.R.3708 - 115th Congress (2017-2018): To Amend the Internal Revenue Code of 1986 to Exclude from Gross Income De Minimis Gains from Certain Sales or Exchanges of Virtual Currency, and for Other Purposes." Congress.gov, 7 Sept. 2017, www.congress.gov/bill/115th-congress/house-bill/3708/text.
[74] "Court Authorizes Service of John Doe Summons Seeking the Identities of U.S. Taxpayers Who Have Used Virtual Currency." The United States Department of Justice, 30 Nov. 2016, www.justice.gov/opa/pr/court-authorizes-service-john-doe-summons-seeking-identities-us-taxpayers-who-have-used.
[75] Brandon, Russell. "Coinbase Ordered to Report 14,355 Users to the IRS." The Verge, The Verge, 29 Nov. 2017, www.theverge.com/2017/11/29/16717416/us-coinbase-irs-records.
[76] Terlato, Peter. "Cryptocurrency Exchange Coinbase Sends Customers Tax Forms." Finder U.S., 10 Apr. 2018, www.finder.com/cryptocurrency-exchange-coinbase-sends-customers-tax-forms.
[77] Benedetti, Hugo and Kostovetsky, Leonard, Digital Tulips? Returns to Investors in Initial Coin Offerings (May 20, 2018). Available at SSRN: https://ssrn.com/abstract=3182169 or http://dx.doi.org/10.2139/ssrn.3182169
[78] "15 U.S. Code § 77b-1 - Swap Agreements." LII / Legal Information Institute, www.law.cornell.edu/uscode/text/15/77b–1.
[79] "SEC v. Howey Co., 328 U.S. 293 (1946)." Justia Law, supreme.justia.com/cases/federal/us/328/293/case.html.
[80] "Report of Investigation Pursuant to Section 21(a) of the Securities Exchange Act of 1934: The DAO." *Securities and Exchange Commission*, United States Securities and Exchange Commission, 25 July 2017, www.sec.gov/litigation/investreport/34-81207.pdf.
[81] Seigel, David. "Understanding The DAO Attack." CoinDesk, CoinDesk, 27 June 2016, www.coindesk.com/understanding-dao-hack-journalists/.
[82] Higgens, Stan. "SEC Chief Clayton: 'Every ICO I've Seen Is a Security'." CoinDesk, CoinDesk, 7 Feb. 2018, www.coindesk.com/sec-chief-clayton-every-ico-ive-seen-security/.
[83] Russo, Camila. "Former CFTC Head Says Big Cryptocurrencies Could Be Classified as Securities." Bloomberg.com, Bloomberg, 23 Apr. 2018, www.bloomberg.com/news/articles/2018-04-23/ether-ripple-may-be-securities-former-cftc-head-gensler-says.
[84] Irrera, Anna, "U.S. SEC official says ether not a security, price surges," Reuters. 14 June. 2018. https://www.reuters.com/article/us-cryptocurrencies-ether/u-s-sec-official-says-ether-not-a-security-price-surges-idUSKBN1JA30Q
[85] Argon Group. "Explaining The 'Simple Agreement For Future Tokens' Framework." Medium, Augmenting Humanity, 29 Nov. 2017, medium.com/@argongroup/explaining-the-simple-agreement-for-future-tokens-framework-15d5e7543323.
[86] "SEC Announces Enforcement Initiatives to Combat Cyber-Based Threats and Protect Retail Investors." *Securities and Exchange Commission*, United States Securities and Exchange Commission, 25 Sept. 2017, www.sec.gov/news/press-release/2017-176.
[87] "Cybersecurity Enforcement Actions." *Securities and Exchange Commission*, United States Securities and Exchange Commission, 20 June 2017, www.sec.gov/spotlight/cybersecurity-enforcement-actions.
[88] "Statement on Potentially Unlawful Online Platforms for Trading Digital Assets." *Securities and Exchange Commission*, United States Securities and Exchange Commission, 7 Mar. 2018, www.sec.gov/news/public-statement/enforcement-tm-statement-potentially-unlawful-online-platforms-trading.
[89] Asiff Hirji, "Our path to listing SEC-regulated crypto securities," The Coinbase Blog 6 June. 2018,

https://blog.coinbase.com/our-path-to-listing-sec-regulated-crypto-securities-a1724e13bb5a

[90] "Fact Sheet: How to Pay at Starbucks." *Starbucks Newsroom*, Starbucks, 22 Nov. 2016, news.starbucks.com/facts/fact-sheet-how-to-pay-at-starbucks.

[91] "Title 12 U.S. Code Chapter 41 - EXPEDITED FUNDS AVAILABILITY." *LII / Legal Information Institute*, Cornell Law School, www.law.cornell.edu/uscode/text/12/chapter-41.

[92] "Regulation CC (Availability of Funds and Collection of Checks)." *Federal Reserve*, United States Federal Reserve System, Board of Governors of the Federal Reserve System, 28 Feb. 2017, www.federalreserve.gov/paymentsystems/regcc-about.htm.

[93] "Public Law 108-100 - Check Clearing for the 21st Century Act." *Government Publishing Office*, United States Government Publishing Office, 28 Oct. 2003, www.gpo.gov/fdsys/pkg/PLAW-108publ100/pdf/PLAW-108publ100.pdf.

[94] "Public Law 111-24 - Credit Card Accountability and Disclosure Act of 2009." *Federal Trade Commission*, United States Federal Trade Commission, 22 May 2009, www.ftc.gov/sites/default/files/documents/statutes/credit-card-accountability-responsibility-and-disclosure-act-2009-credit-card-act/credit-card-pub-l-111-24_0.pdf.

[95] "Truth in Lending Act." *Federal Trade Commission*, United States Federal Trade Commission, 25 July 2016, www.ftc.gov/enforcement/statutes/truth-lending-act.

[96] "Regulation Z: Loan Originator Compensation and Steering - 12 CFR 226." *Federal Reserve System*, United States Federal Reserve System, Board of Governors of the Federal Reserve System, 28 Dec. 2016, www.federalreserve.gov/bankinforeg/regzcg.htm.

[97] "Electronic Fund Transfer Act." *Federal Reserve System*, United States Federal Reserve System, www.federalreserve.gov/boarddocs/caletters/2008/0807/08-07_attachment.pdf.

[98] "2015 FDIC National Survey of Unbanked and Underbanked Households." *Federal Deposit Insurance Corporation*, United States Federal Deposit Insurance Corporation, 20 Oct. 2016, www.fdic.gov/householdsurvey/2015/2015report.pdf.

[99] "2015 FDIC National Survey of Unbanked and Underbanked Households." *Federal Deposit Insurance Corporation*, United States Federal Deposit Insurance Corporation, 20 Oct. 2016, www.fdic.gov/householdsurvey/2015/2015report.pdf.

[100] "CFPB Finalizes Strong Federal Protections for Prepaid Account Consumers." *Consumer Financial Protection Bureau*, United States Consumer Financial Protection Bureau, 5 Oct. 2016, www.consumerfinance.gov/about-us/newsroom/cfpb-finalizes-strong-federal-protections-prepaid-account-consumers/.

[101] "Remittances to Developing Countries Decline for Second Consecutive Year." *World Bank*, The World Bank, 21 Apr. 2017, www.worldbank.org/en/news/press-release/2017/04/21/remittances-to-developing-countries-decline-for-second-consecutive-year.

[102] "Remittance Prices Worldwide." *World Bank*, The World Bank, Mar. 2018, remittanceprices.worldbank.org/sites/default/files/rpw_report_march2018.pdf.

[103] "Electronic Fund Transfers (Regulation E); Amendments." *Consumer Financial Protection Bureau*, United States Consumer Financial Protection Bureau, www.consumerfinance.gov/policy-compliance/rulemaking/final-rules/electronic-fund-transfers-regulation-e/.

[104] "ACH Volume Grows to More Than 25 Billion Payments and $43 Trillion in Value in 2016." *National Automated Clearing House Association*, Automated Clearing House, 12 Apr. 2017, www.nacha.org/news/ach-volume-grows-more-25-billion-payments-and-43-trillion-value-2016.

[105] "Regulation J: Collection of Checks and Other Items by Federal Reserve Banks and Funds Transfers through Fedwire - 12 CFR 2010." *Federal Reserve System*, United States Federal Reserve System, Board of Governors of the Federal Reserve System, 28 Dec. 2016, www.federalreserve.gov/bankinforeg/regjcg.htm.

[106] "CHIPS Rules and Administrative Procedures Effective February 15, 2016." *The Clearing House*, The Clearing House Payments Company L.L.C., Clearing House Association, 2016,

www.theclearinghouse.org/-/media/files/payco%20files/chips%20rules%20and%20administrative%20procedures%202016.pdf?la=en.

[107] United States, Congress, Federal Reserve System. "Regulation CC (Availability of Funds and Collection of Checks)." *Regulation CC (Availability of Funds and Collection of Checks)*, 28 Feb. 2017. www.federalreserve.gov/paymentsystems/regcc-about.htm.

[108] Perez, Sarah. "U.S. Banks' Venmo Alternative, Zelle, Moved $75B Last Year, Says 100,000 People Enroll Daily." *TechCrunch*, TechCrunch, 29 Jan. 2018, techcrunch.com/2018/01/29/u-s-banks-venmo-alternative-zelle-moved-75b-last-year-says-100000-people-enroll-daily/.

[109] "New Protections for Prepaid Accounts." *Consumer Financial Protection Bureau*, United States Consumer Financial Protection Bureau, www.consumerfinance.gov/prepaid-rule/.

[110] "The Fintech 2.0 Paper: Rebooting Financial Services." *Santander Innoventures*, Santander Bank, Oliver Wyman, Anthemis Group, santanderinnoventures.com/wp-content/uploads/2015/06/The-Fintech-2-0-Paper.pdf.

[111] Rosner, Marcel T, and Andrew Kang. "Understanding and Regulating Twenty-First Century Payment Systems: The Ripple Case Study." *University of Michigan Law School Scholarship Repository*, University of Michigan Law School, University of Michigan, repository.law.umich.edu/cgi/viewcontent.cgi?article=1239&context=mlr.

[112] "SWIFT Completes Landmark DLT PoC." *SWIFT*, Society for Worldwide Interbank Financial Telecommunication, 8 Mar. 2018, www.swift.com/news-events/press-releases/swift-completes-landmark-dlt-poc.

[113] Irrera, Anna, and John McCrank. "Wall Street Rethinks Blockchain Projects as Euphoria Meets Reality." *Reuters*, Thomson Reuters, 27 Mar. 2018, www.reuters.com/article/us-banks-fintech-blockchain/wall-street-rethinks-blockchain-projects-as-euphoria-meets-reality-idUSKBN1H32GO.

[114] Irrera, Anna. "JPMorgan Mulls Spin-off of Blockchain Project Quorum: Sources." *Reuters*, Thomson Reuters, 22 Mar. 2018, www.reuters.com/article/us-blockchain-jpmorgan/jpmorgan-mulls-spin-off-of-blockchain-project-quorum-sources-idUSKBN1GY36O.

[115] *Faster Payments Task Force*, Faster Payments Task Force, fasterpaymentstaskforce.org/.

[116] "The U.S. Path to Faster Payments." *Faster Payments Task Force*, Faster Payments Task Force, July 2017, fasterpaymentstaskforce.org/wp-content/uploads/faster-payments-task-force-final-report-part-two.pdf.

[117] "Global Assets under Management Set to Rise to $145.4 Trillion by 2025." *PwC Press Room*, PricewaterhouseCoopers , 30 Oct. 2017, press.pwc.com/News-releases/global-assets-under-management-set-to-rise-to--145.4-trillion-by-2025/s/e236a113-5115-4421-9c75-77191733f15f.

[118] Eule, Alex. "As Robo-Advisors Cross $200 Billion in Assets, Schwab Leads in Performance." *Barron's*, Barron's, 3 Feb. 2018, www.barrons.com/articles/as-robo-advisors-cross-200-billion-in-assets-schwab-leads-in-performance-1517509393.

[119] Eule, Alex. "As Robo-Advisors Cross $200 Billion in Assets, Schwab Leads in Performance." *Barron's*, Barron's, 3 Feb. 2018, www.barrons.com/articles/as-robo-advisors-cross-200-billion-in-assets-schwab-leads-in-performance-1517509393.

[120] Ellis, Charles D. "The End of Active Investing? ." *Financial Times*, The Financial Times, 20 Jan. 2017, www.ft.com/content/6b2d5490-d9bb-11e6-944b-e7eb37a6aa8e.

[121] "Definition of the Term 'Fiduciary'; Conflict of Interest Rule-Retirement Investment Advice." *Federal Register*, The Federal Register, 20 Apr. 2015, www.federalregister.gov/documents/2015/04/20/2015-08831/definition-of-the-term-fiduciary-conflict-of-interest-rule-retirement-investment-advice.

[122] Garmhausen, Steve. "Kiss the DOL Fiduciary Rule Goodbye." *Barron's*, Barron's, 2 May 2018, www.barrons.com/articles/kiss-the-dol-fiduciary-rule-goodbye-1525289845.

[123] "SEC Proposes to Enhance Protections and Preserve Choice for Retail Investors in Their

Relationships With Investment Professionals." *Securities and Exchange Commission*, United States Securities and Exchange Commission, 18 Apr. 2018, www.sec.gov/news/press-release/2018-68.
[124] "Title 17 CFR Part 275 - RULES AND REGULATIONS, INVESTMENT ADVISERS ACT OF 1940." *LII / Legal Information Institute*, Cornell Law School, www.law.cornell.edu/cfr/text/17/part-275.
[125] "IM Guidance Update." *Securities and Exchange Commission*, United States Securities and Exchange Commission, Feb. 2017, www.sec.gov/investment/im-guidance-2017-02.pdf.
[126] "Report on Digital Investment Advice." *Financial Industry Regulatory Authority*, Financial Industry Regulatory Authority, Mar. 2016, www.finra.org/sites/default/files/digital-investment-advice-report.pdf.
[127] "2018 National Exam Program Examination Priorities." *Securities and Exchange Commission*, United States Securities and Exchange Commission, www.sec.gov/about/offices/ocie/national-examination-program-priorities-2018.pdf.
[128] "Financial Technology: Additional Steps by Regulators Could Better Protect Consumers and Aid Regulatory Oversight." *Government Accountability Office*, United States Government Accountability Office, Mar. 2018, www.gao.gov/assets/700/690803.pdf.
[129] "Consumer Protection Principles: Consumer-Authorized Financial Data Sharing and Aggregation." *Consumer Financial Protection Bureau*, The Consumer Financial Protection Bureau, 18 Oct. 2017, files.consumerfinance.gov/f/documents/cfpb_consumer-protection-principles_data-aggregation.pdf
[130] These remarks were made by the member of the Board of Governors of the Federal Reserve System in a personal capacity. Board of Governors of the Federal Reserve System, Remarks by Lael Brainard, Member of the Board of Governors of the Federal Reserve, "Where Do Consumers Fit in the Fintech Stack?" (Ann Arbor, Mich.; November 2017).

[131] Sidel, Robin. "Big Banks Lock Horns With Personal-Finance Web Portals." *The Wall Street Journal*, Dow Jones & Company, 4 Nov. 2015, www.wsj.com/articles/big-banks-lock-horns-with-personal-finance-web-portals-1446683450.
[132] Glazer, Emily, and Peter Rudegeair. "J.P. Morgan, Intuit Give Mint, TurboTax Customers Wider Access to Bank Data." *The Wall Street Journal*, Dow Jones & Company, 25 Jan. 2017, www.wsj.com/articles/j-p-morgan-intuit-give-mint-turbotax-customers-wider-access-to-bank-data-1485340204.